100 Magnificent Muffins & Scones

Felicity Barnum-Bobb

First published in 2006 by Collins
an imprint of HarperCollins Publishers
77–85 Fulham Palace Road
London W6 8JB

The Collins website address is:
www.collins.co.uk

Collins is a registered trademark of
HarperCollins Publishers Ltd

09 08 07 06
9 8 7 6 5 4 3 2 1

A catalogue record for this book is available from the British Library.

ISBN-13 978 0 00 722932 1
ISBN-10 0 00 722932 1

Photographer: Steve Baxter/Marie-Louise Avery
Food and Props Stylist: Felicity Barnum-Bobb
Designer: Nicky Barneby
Senior Commissioning Editor: Jenny Heller
Assistant Editor: Kerenza Swift

Colour reproduction by Colourscan, Singapore
Printed and bound by Printing Express, Hong Kong

100 Magnificent Muffins & Scones

Felicity Barnum-Bobb

Collins

Contents

Introduction

What exactly is a muffin? Is it a cake, bun or type of bread? By working your way through the 100 recipes in this book, you'll discover that it can be all those things. There are muffins and scones here to suit every mood and occasion: sweet and savoury, slimline or indulgent, for a special diet or a special occasion, mini-muffins for children or batch-baking for a party, this book's got it sorted.

American muffins

This book is bursting with recipes for American muffins. Why? Because they are just so easy to make. They taste fantastic and everyone loves them. And best of all, they only take about 30 minutes to make. That's the kind of cooking I go for – deeply satisfying yet speedy. Unlike English muffins (see below), these American treats contain baking powder, the magic ingredient that makes them rise into divine little cakey treats. Don't get led astray by the shop-bought versions, which are always seriously over-sweet – real home-made muffins are never too sweet and they can, of course, be savoury too.

English muffins

The word 'muffin' is thought to have come from an old French word 'moufflet', meaning soft and referring to bread. There are references to English muffin recipes as early as 1747, but they were most popular in the nineteenth century.

Making English muffins is quite time-consuming because they use yeast. Although my recipes use easy-blend yeast to speed things up, you still need to leave the dough to rise. I don't know about you, but when I'm baking I'm usually looking for instant gratification and I want the process to be fast and easy. My solution is to use a bread maker. Throw all the ingredients in the machine in the order your manufacturer recommends and let it do all the hard work, kneading and proving the dough. Then all you have to do is shape and cook them. Cooking English muffins is different – you don't bake them, they are cooked on a hotplate or a solid flat griddle (an Aga hotplate is perfect) which gives them their traditional flat tops and bottoms. It'll take a few attempts to get them cooked to perfection, but it's worth persevering.

If you have children to entertain (as I regularly do, being a mother of four), I thoroughly recommend making the muffins by hand together. Measuring out the ingredients is a maths lesson in itself, and giving each child responsibility for one ingredient will make the whole thing a great team effort. Once the bulk of the dough is made, divide it equally between the children and let them each knead a piece. The great thing about any yeast mixture is the more you manhandle it, the better the end result will be. Encourage them to vent their anger on the dough, rather than each other, punch it, poke and smash it on the table. Even throwing the dough's fine, as long as it's not aimed at someone else!

Scones

These are speedy to make as they use self-raising flour or baking powder as their raising agent. This Scottish quick bread is said to have taken its name from the Stone of Destiny (or Scone), the place where Scottish kings were once crowned. The original recipe was made with oats and griddle baked. My recipes are more flour-based and are all baked in a hot oven for ease. They come in various shapes, but most commonly as rounds. There is a lot of debate over the pronunciation of the word. It's suggested that if you're posh you say 'skown' to rhyme with 'cone' while less privileged people say 'skon' to rhyme with 'gone'! I say that's nonsense, and all that matters is that you enjoy baking and eating them.

Shortcut secrets

You really don't need any fancy equipment to make up these recipes – a large bowl, measuring jug, sieve, wooden spoon and a muffin tray will suffice. However, because I'm usually multi-tasking (feeding the children and baking), I sometimes use a freestanding mixer. They will gently combine the dry ingredients with the wet and won't over-mix if used on the lowest setting (which is a good thing, as it can make American-style muffins heavy).

When you need to get your skates on and produce something quickly, get out the food processor and it will charge through the recipe in a matter of minutes – and because you're so short of time you won't over-mix. Those are the times when you can forget sieving the flour and it really won't matter – the muffins will taste fine! Use the microwave to melt the butter – 30–50 seconds on high (850w) and it's softened enough to use. Use the processor or a coffee grinder to chop nuts speedily.

When the pressure's on always line the muffin tins with paper cases as you can always peel them off to serve. There's no need to worry about cooling the muffins on a wire rack – if they're in the paper cases, they're fine to cool in the tins.

That fresh-baked taste

If you're going to the hassle of doing the home-made thing, you'll want everything to taste as good as possible. We're so used to shop-bought goods having a long shelf-life that it's easy to forget that these muffins will only stay fresh for a couple of days. The solution? Pop extra muffins into the freezer and reheat in the microwave to serve. One muffin will take 30 seconds on high (850w) to reheat from frozen. Another option is to make up the mixture and leave it in the fridge overnight. You could bake half of the muffins on one day and the remainder the next. If you have plenty of space in your freezer and a muffin tin to spare, why not freeze the unbaked muffins in their cases in the tin? Bake from frozen for an extra 5 minutes.

Essential tips for successful baking

- Invest in a set of cook's measuring spoons. Household spoons vary so much in size, so results are not consistent. These recipes were tested with the following measuring spoons:

  5ml = 1tsp, 10ml = 2 tsp, 15ml = 1tbsp.

  All spoon measurements should be level.

- Prepare recipes entirely in metric or imperial – never switch between the two whilst following a recipe.

- Always set your scales to zero when you measure.

- Check liquid measurements in a jug at eye level, or use digital scales which measure liquids too.

- Allow melted butter to cool for a few minutes before mixing with eggs.

- All eggs are medium unless otherwise stated.

- If using a conventional oven, always bake muffins and scones towards the top of the oven.

- To cook in a fan oven, reduce oven temperatures by 20°C otherwise the muffins will burn (see chart on p.8). Any rack in the oven is suitable since the temperature is even throughout.

- Test for doneness by inserting a cocktail stick into the centre of the muffins – it should come out clean.

Oven temperature conversions

Conventional oven	Fan oven	Gas mark	Aga 2 oven	Aga 4 oven
170°C/325°F	140°C	3	Roasting oven – lower shelf with grid shelf on base and plain shelf above	Baking oven – bottom shelf
180°C/350°F	160°C	4	Roasting oven – lower shelf with grid shelf on base and plain shelf above	Baking oven – bottom shelf
190°C/375°F	170°C	5	Roasting oven – lower shelf with grid shelf on base and plain shelf above	Baking oven – bottom shelf
200°C/400°F	180°C	6	Roasting oven – lower shelf with grid shelf on base and plain shelf above	Baking oven – bottom shelf
220°C/425°F	200°C	7	Roasting oven – lowest shelf with grid shelf on base	Baking oven – top shelf
230°C/450°F	210°C	8	Roasting oven – third shelf	Baking oven – third shelf

Cooking in a fan oven is generally 25% faster than in a conventional oven.

For Aga baking, ingredients such as butter can be softened or melted in the simmering oven. Drop scones etc can be cooked directly on the simmering plate. Lightly grease the plate before cooking.

Baking tin sizes

The muffins in this book come in three different sizes: regular, mini and mega.

Most of the recipes use a regular muffin tin (100ml/ 4fl oz); each hole measures 5cm (2in) at the base, 7cm (2¾in) at the top and is 3cm (1¼in) deep.

Mega-muffins (150ml/5lf oz) are cooked in tins measuring 6cm (2½in) at the base, 8½cm (3½in) at the top and 4cm (1¾in) deep.

Mini-muffin tins (30ml/2 tbsp) measure 3cm (1¼in) at the base, 4.5cm (1¾in) at the top and are 2cm (¾in) deep. Line them with mini-muffin cases (also sold as mini cake cases). When testing the recipes for the children's chapter, I discovered that these mini ones are absolutely weeny, so on occasions I recommend using a patty tin (50ml/2fl oz) of the type usually used to make fairy cakes. These measure 4cm (1½in) at the base, 6cm (2½in) at the top and are 2cm (¾in) deep. Line with baking cases.

I suggest you invest in a mini-muffin tin, a regular muffin tin, a mega muffin tin and a patty tin and you'll then be equipped to bake any of the muffin recipes in this book.

Troubleshooting

Although I've tested and re-tested all the recipes in this book to make sure they work, there's always a chance that the end result might not meet your expectations. If you think something has gone wrong, check out the possible causes and solutions below.

Under-baked and slightly sunken?

It is likely that the oven had not reached the correct temperature before the muffins or scones were put in the oven. Always pre-heat the oven at the beginning of a recipe and only put the goodies in to bake when the light goes out, indicating the correct temperature has been reached.

How to fix it: If you realise that the muffins are under-cooked and sinking within 30 minutes of taking them out of the oven, you could return them to the hot oven and cook for a few more minutes. If you don't realise for an hour or so, try microwaving a few at a time. Cook on high (850w) for 1 minute, leave to stand for a couple of minutes, then test with a cocktail stick – it should come out clean.

Over-baked?

Was the oven temperature set correctly? Did you use the right size muffin tins and not smaller patty (fairy cake) tins? If you have a fan oven, you need to adjust the temperature accordingly, baking 20 degrees lower than a conventional oven (see oven temperatures chart opposite). Or is your oven 10 or 20 degrees hotter than the oven indicates? If you find things regularly burn, call out a service engineer from the cooker's manufacturer – they can test your oven to check that it is correctly calibrated.

How to fix it: How over-baked are they? Burnt tops need to be cut off. Disguise with icing, melted chocolate or cream cheese frosting. If they're not burnt, but just a little dry, pierce a few times with a cocktail stick and drizzle some fruit juice or booze over sweet muffins. Drizzle savoury muffins with olive oil.

Crusty top?

This is usually caused if you've used too much sugar. Did you measure it carefully? Did you measure the golden syrup accurately? Digital scales that you can set to zero with each ingredient make adding ingredients directly to the mixing bowl easier. Also, use a measuring spoon dipped in hot water to make sure the syrup doesn't cling to the spoon.

How to fix it: Dust the tops with icing sugar to taste like an intentional sugary crust.

Fruit sank?

Did you gently toss the fruit in the flour before adding the wet ingredients? This is a critical stage. Also, was the oven pre-heated to the correct temperature? If it is too low, the mixture does not set quickly enough to support the fruit while the mixture bakes.

How to fix it: Nothing you can do, but remember these hints for next time.

Muffin tops cracked and not baked through?

This is caused when the oven is too hot, so the top bakes quickly and sets before the lower part of the muffin has cooked, then during baking the mixture underneath forces its way up as it bakes and rises, splitting the already set surface.

How to fix it: Dust with icing sugar.

Flat tops that didn't rise properly?

Did you remember to put in the correct amount of raising agent ? Measure baking powder and bicarbonate of soda carefully with a measuring spoon – exact quantities are critical for the muffins to rise successfully. Also check the packets to ensure that the raising agents haven't passed their use-by date.

How to fix it: Cover with icing and call them cup cakes!

Muffins too crumbly?

If the mixture is quite stiff when it goes in to bake, the end result will probably be dry and crumbly. Measure liquids and fats carefully. If the texture is too crumbly, not enough liquid was added.

How to fix it: Drizzle with a lemon sugar syrup, some booze or fruit juice.

Oily texture?

Did you use butter or the oil suggested in the recipe? It sounds like you tried to use a low-fat spread or margarine. These contain water, and have the weird effect of separating out during cooking and making the muffin texture oily.

How to fix it: Serve with tangy fruit for sweet muffins or a crisp vinegar-dressed salad for savoury ones.

Dense texture?

Sounds like you may have over-mixed. Stir the wet and dry ingredients together for about ten strokes until everything is just combined. Don't over-mix.

How to fix it: Microwave individual muffins and serve warm, like a pudding. Serve with ice cream or custard to disguise.

Seriously sunken? (pictured)

You've added too much raising agent. Use measuring spoons for accuracy.

How to fix it: Put some raspberries on top!

Mixture overflows?

Did you use large eggs instead of medium? (All recipes use medium eggs unless large are specified.) Have you used the correct size of muffin tin?

How to fix it: Make sure next time you only spoon enough muffin mixture into the cases or tin holes so that they are two-thirds full.

Cooked unevenly?

Are some of the muffins browned, whilst others are not? Sounds like your oven is cooking unevenly.

How to fix it: Next time, turn muffins round after 10–15 minutes cooking time, but don't open the oven door too soon or they'll sink.

Muffins sticking to tins?

Did you grease them thoroughly? Use butter or sunflower oil and make sure you smear it right into the corners. Were you too impatient getting them out of the tins? Leave in the tins for 10 minutes to cool and firm up – if you try to remove them too soon, they'll be too fragile and break up. However, if you leave them too long they may well set in the tins.

How to fix it: Ideally use a non-stick tin, or a flexible plastic one. Use a palette knife to ease around the sides of each muffin and gently slip underneath to release. Or use paper muffin cases every time – they make life a lot easier.

Brilliant for Breakfast

Baking something for breakfast may sound like I'm living in cloud cuckoo-land. I know people lead busy lives and there's barely enough time to grab a slice of toast most days. What about weekends or birthdays or when you have friends to stay? If you're more energetic in the evenings than mornings, weigh out the ingredients before you go to bed and then the following day, turn on the oven, mix together the ingredients and in no time you can tuck into warm, home-baked delights. And once you've made a batch, extras can be frozen and microwaved individually as and when you fancy a treat.

Granary honey muffins

Just because these look like cakes doesn't mean they're going to taste like cakes! They're nothing like any shop-bought super-sweet specimen – in fact they're almost as savoury as a good old-fashioned slice of toast.

1 Heat the oven to 200°C/400°F/gas 6. Line a muffin tin with 9 muffin cases.
2 Tip the flour into a large bowl. Add the baking powder and sugar.
3 Mix together the honey, oil, egg, lemon zest and milk and pour into the dry ingredients in the bowl. Use a large spoon to fold everything together.
4 Spoon equally into the paper muffin cases and bake for 15 minutes until the muffins are well risen, firm and springy to the touch. Serve warm.

MAKES 9 / READY IN 30 MINUTES

200g | 7oz malted brown flour
15ml | 1 tbsp baking powder
25g | 1oz light muscovado sugar
45ml | 3 tbsp runny honey
100ml | 4fl oz sunflower oil
1 medium egg
Finely grated zest of 1 small lemon
150ml | 5fl oz skimmed milk

Five-seed muffins

Bursting with goodness – what better way to start your day?

1 Heat the oven to 200°C/400°F/gas 6. Line a 12-hole muffin tin with paper muffin cases.
2 Sift the white flour into a large bowl. Add the wholemeal flour, baking powder, all the seeds, raisins and sugar.
3 Mix together the oil, egg and milk and pour into the dry ingredients in the bowl.
Stir together with a large spoon until just combined.
4 Spoon equally into the paper muffin cases and sprinkle with a fine dusting of your chosen seeds.
5 Bake for 15 minutes until the muffins are well risen, firm and springy to the touch. Serve warm.

MAKES 12 / READY IN 30 MINUTES

125g | 4 oz self-raising white flour
125g | 4 oz stone-ground wholemeal flour
15ml | 1 tbsp baking powder
50g | 2oz mixture of linseeds, poppy, sesame, sunflower and pumpkin seeds
125g | 4oz raisins
75g | 3oz light muscovado sugar
100ml | 4fl oz sunflower oil
1 medium egg
150ml | 5fl oz skimmed milk
Extra seeds, for dusting

Apricot and oat muffins

These are great for freezing (see Cook's tip below), so make a batch of 12, then eat a few and freeze the remainder.

MAKES 12 / READY IN 30 MINUTES

125g | 4oz self-raising white flour
100g | 3½oz wholemeal flour
15ml | 1 tbsp baking powder
75g | 3oz rolled oats
175g | 6oz dried apricots, chopped
125g | 4oz sultanas
75g | 3oz light muscovado sugar
100ml | 4fl oz sunflower oil
1 medium egg
Finely grated zest and juice of 1 orange
150ml | 5fl oz skimmed milk
Extra rolled oats, for sprinkling

1 Heat the oven to 200°C/400°F/gas 6. Line a 12-hole muffin tin with paper muffin cases.
2 Sift the white flour into a large bowl. Add the wholemeal flour, baking powder, rolled oats, apricots, sultanas and sugar.
3 Mix together the oil, egg, orange zest, juice and milk and pour into the dry ingredients in the bowl. Use a large spoon to fold everything together.

4 Spoon equally into the paper muffin cases and sprinkle with oats.
5 Bake for 15 minutes until the muffins are well risen, firm and springy to the touch. Serve warm.

Cook's tip: To freeze the muffins, cool completely and pack in small plastic bags. To serve, microwave on high (850w) for 40 seconds to warm through one muffin.

Wholemeal apple

Try these for a tasty yet healthy high-fibre start to the day.

MAKES 12 / READY IN 30 MINUTES

75g | 3oz self-raising white flour
150g | 6oz wholemeal flour
15ml | 1 tbsp baking powder
2.5ml | ½ tsp ground cinnamon
75g | 3oz dried apples, chopped
100g | 3½oz sultanas
75g | 3oz light muscovado sugar
100ml | 4fl oz sunflower oil
1 medium egg
150ml | 5fl oz skimmed milk
30ml | 2 tbsp rolled oats, for sprinkling

1 Heat the oven to 200°C/400°F/gas 6. Line a 12-hole muffin tin with paper muffin cases.
2 Sift the white flour into a large bowl. Add the wholemeal flour, baking powder, cinnamon, apples, sultanas and sugar.
3 Mix together the oil, egg and milk and pour into the dry ingredients in the bowl.

Use a large spoon to mix everything together until just combined.
4 Spoon equally into the paper muffin cases and sprinkle with oats.
5 Bake for 15 minutes until the muffins are well risen, firm and springy to the touch. Serve warm.

English muffins

These traditional muffins are entirely different to American-style muffins baked in paper cases. The recipe uses a yeast dough so they take longer to make. I've used easy-blend yeast to save a little time, or see the Cook's tips for using a bread machine. These are traditionally served at teatime, but I think they make a really special treat for breakfast.

MAKES 8–10 / READY IN 1 HOUR 15 MINUTES

450g | 1lb strong white bread flour
5ml | 1 tsp salt
50g | 2oz butter, plus extra for greasing
7g sachet easy-blend dried yeast
5ml | 1 tsp golden caster sugar
250ml | 8fl oz warm milk

1 Sift the flour and salt into a bowl. Microwave on medium (500W) for 1 minute, to warm slightly (there's no need to warm the flour if you don't have a microwave – it simply helps the yeast to work faster).

2 Melt the butter in a bowl in the microwave for 50 seconds on high (850w), or in a pan.

3 Add the easy-blend yeast and sugar to the warm flour. Pour in the warm milk and butter.

4 Beat well until smooth and elastic. Cover and leave to rise in a warm place for 30 minutes or until doubled in size.

5 Turn onto a well-floured board and knead, working in a little more flour if necessary to make the dough easier to shape. Round up the dough, roll into a thick sausage shape and (using the sharpest knife you have) slice into 8–10 portions, each about 3cm | 1½in thick.

6 Use a plain cutter to help shape each one into a round with straight sides. Place on a greased baking sheet, well spaced out. Cover with greased plastic wrap and put in a warm place to prove for 30–40 minutes or until springy to the touch.

7 Heat a griddle until really hot, grease lightly with butter. Lift the muffins carefully onto the hot griddle and cook a few at a time over very low heat for 8–10 minutes until pale golden underneath. Turn and cook the other side.

8 Wrap in a cloth and keep warm if cooking in batches. To serve, insert a knife in the side, pull the top and bottom slightly apart, and insert slivers of butter.

Cook's tips

● Mix the dough with a heavy-duty electric mixer or, if you have a bread machine, you can just use it to knead and prove dough, then you can shape and bake it conventionally.

● Leave the dough to rise in a warm place, such as on the hob whilst the oven's on or in the airing cupboard.

● Speed up the proving by microwaving the dough on defrost for 2 minutes.

● Freeze half the shaped dough before baking. Bake from frozen (just add a few more minutes to the cooking time).

How to adapt recipes for a bread machine:

Check your instruction booklet as there is usually a very specific order in which you must add the ingredients to the bread bucket. Adding the ingredients in the wrong order could cause the recipe to fail. Most machines need liquid added first, followed by dry ingredients, then yeast. Confusingly, a few models use the reverse order. This is important for machines that have a rest time before the cycle starts as the yeast must be kept separate from the liquid, sugar and salt.

Bacon, cheese and maple syrup

I love American breakfasts – they're so indulgent and the tradition of combining savoury and sweet flavours on one plate for breakfast is great. Try these muffins and I bet you'll become hooked.

MAKES 8 / READY IN 30 MINUTES

4 rashers smoked back bacon, chopped

175g | 6oz self-raising flour

5ml | 1 tsp baking powder

1.25ml | ¼ tsp salt

50g | 2oz mature Cheddar cheese, grated

75ml | 3fl oz sunflower oil

1 medium egg

6oml | 4 tbsp maple syrup

150ml | 5fl oz skimmed milk

1 Heat the oven to 200°C/400°F/gas 6. Line a muffin tin with 8 paper cases.
2 Microwave the bacon uncovered on an ovenproof plate on high (850w) for 3 minutes until cooked and becoming crispy. (Or dry-fry in a non-stick frying pan.)
3 Sift the flour, baking powder and salt into a bowl. Stir in the bacon and cheese. Make a well in the centre.
4 Pour the oil, egg, half the maple syrup and the milk into a jug, mix together, then pour into the well, in the centre. Mix together briefly until just combined.
5 Spoon the mixture into the prepared muffin cases and bake for 15 minutes until risen, firm and a cocktail stick inserted into the centre comes out clean.
6 Serve warm, drizzled with the remaining maple syrup.

Cook's tip: Cool and freeze for up to 1 month. Defrost one muffin at a time in the microwave on high (850W) for 40 seconds.

Muesli muffins

Wholesome and satisfying served just as they are.

MAKES 9 / READY IN 30 MINUTES

50g | 2oz self-raising white flour

75g | 3oz wholemeal flour

10ml | 2 tsp baking powder

100g | 3½oz fruit-and-nut muesli

50g | 2oz raisins

75g | 3oz light muscovado sugar

100ml | 4fl oz sunflower oil

1 medium egg

150ml | 5fl oz skimmed milk

Extra muesli, for dusting

1 Heat the oven to 200°C/400°F/gas 6. Line a muffin tin with 9 paper muffin cases.
2 Sift the white flour into a large bowl. Add the wholemeal flour, baking powder, muesli, raisins and sugar.
3 Mix together the oil, egg and milk in a jug, then pour into the dry ingredients in the bowl. Use a large metal spoon to fold everything together.
4 Spoon evenly into the paper muffin cases, sprinkle with the extra muesli and bake for 15 minutes until the muffins are well risen, firm and springy to the touch. Serve warm.

Smoked salmon and soured cream

For a very refined yet substantial breakfast, try these muffins served with scrambled eggs. Alternatively, bake them as mini-muffins and serve them with pre-dinner drinks or as part of a buffet.

1 Heat the oven to 200°C/400°F/gas 6. Line a muffin tin with 9 paper muffin cases (or line mini-muffin tins with 24 mini-muffin paper cases).
2 Sift the flour, baking powder and salt into a bowl. Stir in the smoked salmon, chives and cheese. Make a well in the centre.

3 Pour the oil, egg, mustard and milk into the well. Mix together briefly until just combined.
4 Spoon the mixture into the prepared muffin cases and bake for 12 minutes until risen, firm and a cocktail stick inserted into the centre comes out clean. (Mini-muffins should be baked for 7 minutes.)

MAKES 9, OR 24 MINI-MUFFINS / READY IN 30 MINUTES

225g | 8oz self-raising flour
5ml | 1 tsp baking powder
1.25ml | ¼ tsp salt
75g | 3oz smoked salmon trimmings, chopped
15ml | 1 tbsp freshly chopped chives, optional
25g | 1oz Parmesan cheese, grated
75ml | 3fl oz sunflower oil
1 medium egg, lightly beaten
15ml | 1 tbsp wholegrain mustard
150ml | 5fl oz skimmed milk

Marmalade orange muffins

Split and fill these with a dollop of marmalade, if you crave that extra degree of sweetness, to start your day.

1 Heat the oven to 200°C/400°F/gas 6. Line a 12-hole muffin tin with paper muffin cases.
2 Sift the white flour into a large bowl. Add the malted brown flour, baking powder and sugar.
3 Mix together the marmalade, oil, egg, orange zest, juice and milk and pour into the dry ingredients in the bowl. Use a large metal spoon to fold everything together.

4 Spoon equally into the paper muffin cases.
5 Bake for 15 minutes until the muffins are well risen, firm and springy to the touch. Serve warm.

Cook's tip: To freeze the muffins, cool completely and pack in small plastic bags. To defrost, microwave one muffin at a time on high (850w) for 30 seconds.

MAKES 12 / READY IN 30 MINUTES

150g | 5oz self-raising white flour
150g | 5oz malted brown flour
15ml | 1 tbsp baking powder
75g | 3oz light muscovado sugar
100g | 3½ oz marmalade
100ml | 4fl oz sunflower oil
1 medium egg
Finely grated zest and juice of 1 orange
75ml | 3fl oz skimmed milk

Muscovado, bran and banana

'Muscovado' describes a type of brown sugar that's unrefined as it comes directly from sugar cane grown in Mauritius, giving it a gorgeous caramelly flavour. Taste a few grains of muscovado sugar, then do the same with regular brown sugar – you'll notice the difference in flavour. Brown sugars that are not labelled muscovado are fully refined white sugars that have had some molasses added – nowhere near as yummy. These muffins are high in fibre and are satisfyingly filling.

MAKES 12 / READY IN 35 MINUTES

200g | 7oz plain wholemeal flour

50g | 2oz bran

45ml | 3tbsp light muscovado sugar

30ml | 2 tsp baking powder

Pinch of salt

100g | 3½oz raisins

150ml | 5fl oz milk

1 large egg

75ml | 3fl oz sunflower oil

2 ripe bananas, peeled (225g | 8oz peeled weight)

1 Pre-heat the oven to 200°C/400°F/gas 6. Line a 12-hole muffin tin with paper muffin cases.
2 Mix the flour, bran, sugar, baking powder, salt and raisins together in a bowl.
3 In a jug lightly whisk together the milk, egg and oil with a fork. Pour the wet ingredients onto the dry ingredients and gently stir together until just blended.
4 Mash up the bananas with a fork and add to the muffin mixture. Don't over mix.
5 Spoon the mixture evenly into the muffin cases and bake for 20–25 minutes or until a cocktail stick inserted into the centre of one comes out clean.

Children's Choice

Yes, we all know children love sweet things, but that doesn't mean we need to pump them full of artificial sweeteners, colourings and additives to present them with fun food. These muffins will help satisfy their cravings for something naughty without compromising your food standards. Because many of these may well be made for birthday parties, or for when friends come round, I've kept the muffin size small. Why waste big muffins on little appetites when you can make them mini? If they're a hit the children can come back for more.

Chocolate chip muffins

Let your imagination go to give you endless variations on this recipe. Although I suggest chocolate chips, why not substitute your favourite chocolate of the moment. If you like chocolates with a honeycomb centre or squidgy toffee, they're worth a try. Cut them into tiny chunks, the size of your little fingernail (you may find it less messy doing this if they've been chilled a little first), then you can be the judge of how successful your chosen confectionery is.

MAKES 12 PATTY TIN SIZED MUFFINS / READY IN 30 MINUTES

150g | 5oz plain flour

5ml | 1 tsp baking powder

75g | 3oz golden caster sugar

50g | 2oz milk chocolate chips

150 ml | 5fl oz soured cream

1 medium egg

60ml | 4 tbsp sunflower oil

1 Pre-heat the oven to 190°C/375°F/gas 5. Line a 12-hole patty tin with paper cases.
2 Sift the flour and baking powder into a bowl and add the sugar and chocolate chips and stir to combine.
3 Put the soured cream, egg and sunflower oil into a jug and mix together with a fork until smooth.

4 Stir the wet ingredients into the dry until just combined.
5 Spoon the mixture into the paper cases and bake for 6-8 minutes until the muffins are well risen, pale golden and a cocktail stick inserted into the centre comes out clean.

Crunchy peanut butter muffins

Before you offer these to any children, do check that they're not allergic to nuts.

MAKES 24 MINI-MUFFINS / READY IN 25 MINUTES

150g | 5oz plain flour

5ml | 1 tsp baking powder

100g | 3½oz golden caster sugar

Pinch of salt

90ml | 6 tbsp crunchy peanut butter

100 ml | 4fl oz sunflower oil

1 large egg

175ml | 6fl oz skimmed milk

1 Pre-heat the oven to 200°C/400°F/gas 6. Line mini-muffin tins with 24 paper mini-muffin cases.
2 Sieve the flour, baking powder, sugar and salt together into a bowl.
3 In a large jug mix the peanut butter, oil, egg and milk together with a fork.

4 Pour the wet ingredients into the dry, stir gently together to combine.
5 Spoon into the paper muffin cases. Bake for 7 minutes or until the muffins are firm, risen and golden, and a cocktail stick inserted into the centre comes out clean.

Banana and honey muffins

This is a great way to use up over-ripe bananas. Because the bananas are squishy, you can get away with not using any eggs.

MAKES 24 MINI-MUFFINS / READY IN 30 MINUTES

150g | 5oz plain flour
7.5ml | 1½ tsp baking powder
2.5ml | ½ tsp bicarbonate of soda
1.25ml | ¼ tsp ground cinnamon
75 ml | 3fl oz sunflower oil
6oml | 4 tbsp runny honey
5oml | 2fl oz semi-skimmed milk
2 small ripe bananas, peeled and mashed (150g | 6oz peeled weight)

1 Heat the oven to 190°C/375°F/gas 5. Line 24 mini-muffin tins with paper mini-muffin cases.
2 Sieve the flour, baking powder, bicarbonate of soda and cinnamon into a bowl.
3 In a large jug, mix together the oil, honey and milk with a fork.
4 Pour the wet ingredients onto the dry and gently stir together with the mashed bananas.
5 Spoon into the mini-muffin cases and bake for 8-10 minutes until risen and firm.
6 Eat whilst warm or cool on a wire rack.

Cook's tip: Whiz up the bananas with a hand blender for a speedy way to make them really smooth.

Chocolate muffins

These have a sweeter taste rather than being really chocolatey, and are so easy that children can make them too.

MAKES 17 PATTY TIN SIZED MUFFINS / READY IN 25 MINUTES

100g | 3½oz butter
225g | 8oz plain flour
30ml | 2 tbsp cocoa
15ml | 1 tbsp baking powder
125g | 4oz light muscovado sugar
Pinch of salt
1 large egg
300ml | 10fl oz natural yogurt
90ml | 6 tbsp chocolate spread
45ml | 3 tbsp chocolate-flavoured hundreds and thousands

1 Pre-heat the oven to 200°C/400°F/gas 6. Line patty tins with 17 paper cases.
2 Melt the butter in a jug in the microwave for 50 seconds on high (850w), or in a pan over a low heat.
3 Sieve together the flour, cocoa and baking powder into a bowl. Add the sugar and salt.
4 Add the egg and yogurt to the melted butter and mix with a fork. Mix the wet ingredients with the dry.
5 Spoon into the paper cases. Bake for 10-15 minutes until the muffins are risen and firm.
6 Cool the muffins on a wire rack. When cool, top with chocolate spread and smooth over to cover. Sprinkle with hundreds and thousands to finish.

Coconut muffins

These coconut muffins are topped with a smothering of jam and a scattering of tenderised sweetened coconut. The ordinary desiccated variety would do, but it doesn't have quite the same 'yum' factor. As an alternative, top the finished muffins with chocolate spread instead of jam before crowning them with a sprinkling from tropical heaven.

MAKES 24 MINI-MUFFINS / READY IN 30 MINUTES

150g | 5oz plain flour

5ml | 1 tsp baking powder

75g | 3oz golden caster sugar

50g | 2oz sweetened tenderised coconut

150ml | 5fl oz tropical-flavoured yogurt

1 medium egg

60ml | 4 tbsp sunflower oil

To decorate:

45ml | 3 tbsp strawberry jam

45ml | 3 tbsp sweetened tenderised coconut

1 Heat the oven to 190°C/375°F/gas 5. Line mini-muffin tins with 24 paper mini-muffin cases.

2 Sift the flour and baking powder into a bowl, add the sugar and sweetened tenderised coconut and stir to combine.

3 Put the tropical yogurt, egg and sunflower oil into a jug and mix together with a fork until smooth.

4 Stir the wet ingredients into the dry until just combined.

5 Spoon the mixture into the paper muffin cases and bake for 6–8 minutes until the muffins are well risen, pale golden and firm.

6 Brush over the strawberry jam whilst warm and sprinkle over the remaining sweetened tenderised coconut, to decorate.

Lemon curd muffins

If you splash out on a slightly more expensive, better quality brand of lemon curd, it'll be worth it as the muffins will have a more defined lemony flavour that even children will detect. These are fab eaten warm.

MAKES 12 PATTY TIN SIZED MUFFINS / READY IN 30 MINUTES

200g | 7oz self-raising flour

100g | 3½oz golden caster sugar

1 large egg

75ml | 3fl oz sunflower oil

150 ml | 5fl oz milk

2.5ml | ½ tsp vanilla extract

60ml | 12 tsp lemon curd

For the sugar coating:

60ml | 4 tbsp lemon curd

50g | 2oz golden caster sugar

1 Heat the oven to 190°C/375°F/gas 5. Line a 12-hole patty tin with paper cases.

2 Sieve the flour into a bowl and stir in the sugar.

3 In a large jug mix together the egg, sunflower oil, milk and vanilla extract, using a fork.

4 Pour the wet ingredients into the dry and stir gently together until just combined.

5 Put a teaspoonful of the mixture in the base of each paper case. Top with 5ml | 1 tsp lemon curd. Top with the rest of the muffin mixture.

6 Bake for 10–15 minutes until risen and firm.

7 For the sugar coating, microwave the lemon curd on high (850w) for 1 minute until melted. Put the sugar into a shallow bowl. Brush on top of each muffin and dip the top of each one in the sugar to coat the tops.

Pink fairy muffins

These fairy dust-topped buns are such a pretty shade of pink, yet there's not a smidgen of food colouring in sight.

1 Heat the oven to 190°C/375°F/gas 5. Line a 12-hole mini-muffin tin with paper mini-muffin cases.
2 Sift the flour and baking powder into a bowl, add the sugar and dried cherries and stir to combine.
3 Put the strawberry yogurt, jam, egg and sunflower oil into a jug and mix together with a fork until smooth.

4 Stir the wet ingredients into the dry until just combined.
5 Spoon the mixture into the paper cases and bake for 6-8 minutes until the muffins are firm and well risen.
6 Mix together the jam and granulated sugar and sprinkle on top of each muffin to look like fairy dust.
7 Decorate with a mini paper fairy secured onto a cocktail stick.

MAKES 12 MINI-MUFFINS / READY IN 30 MINUTES

150g | 5oz plain flour
5ml | 1 tsp baking powder
75g | 3oz golden caster sugar
50g | 2oz dried sour cherries
150ml | 5fl oz strawberry yogurt
15ml | 1 tbsp strawberry jam
1 medium egg
60ml | 4 tbsp sunflower oil

To decorate:
20ml | 4 tsp strawberry jam
45ml | 3 tbsp granulated sugar

Marbled soccer muffins

Every boy's fantasy. There's no food colouring in these either to make those boisterous chaps uncontrollable.

1 Heat the oven to 190°C/375°F/gas 5. Line a 12-hole mini-muffin tin with paper cases.
2 Sift the flour and baking powder into a bowl, add the sugar and stir to combine.
3 Put the egg and sunflower oil into a jug and mix together with a fork until smooth.
4 Stir the wet ingredients into the dry until just combined.
5 Spoon half of the mixture into another bowl. Stir the chocolate fromage frais and cocoa into one bowl and the vanilla fromage frais into the other bowl.

6 Spoon a dollop of each mixture alternately into the muffin cases and bake for 6-8 minutes until the muffins are firm and well risen.
7 Melt the white chocolate in a bowl over simmering water or microwave on medium (500w) for 2 minutes. Pour the melted chocolate over the cooled muffins.
8 Trim off the corners of the chocolate buttons to make hexagons and arrange three on top of each muffin.

MAKES 12 MINI-MUFFINS / READY IN 30 MINUTES

150g | 5oz plain flour
5ml | 1 tsp baking powder
75g | 3oz golden caster sugar
1 medium egg, lightly beaten
60ml | 4 tbsp sunflower oil
2 x 60ml pots chocolate fromage frais
2 tsp cocoa
2 x 60ml pots vanilla fromage frais

To decorate:
100g | 3½oz white chocolate, broken into squares
36 milk chocolate buttons

Jam surprise muffins

There's something almost doughnutty about these muffins with their jammy centres. For the best results, eat them warm.

1 Heat the oven to 190°C/375°F/gas 5. Line a 12-hole patty tin with paper cases. Next sieve the flour into a bowl and stir in the sugar.

2 In a large jug mix together the egg, sunflower oil, milk and vanilla extract, using a fork.

3 Pour the wet ingredients into the dry and stir gently together until just combined.

4 Put a teaspoonful of the mixture in the base of each paper case. Top with a dollop of strawberry jam. Top with the rest of the muffin mixture.

5 Bake for 10 minutes until well risen and firm.

6 Put the sugar in a shallow bowl. Brush the tops with melted butter and dip in the sugar to coat the tops.

MAKES 12 PATTY TIN SIZED MUFFINS / READY IN 30 MINUTES

200g | 7oz self-raising flour
100g | 3½oz golden caster sugar
1 large egg
75 ml | 3fl oz sunflower oil
150 ml | 5fl oz milk
2.5ml | ½ tsp vanilla extract
40ml | 8 tsp strawberry jam

For the sugar coating:
25g | 1oz unsalted butter, melted
25g | 1oz golden caster sugar

Squashed fly muffins

Do you remember 'squashed fly' biscuits as a child? I loved those crisp, thin biscuit bars with a generous portion of currants. I fall into the group who think of dried fruit as the cherry on top of the cake; something of a treat to savour. My children don't feel the same way as I do and tend to think of anything containing raisins as a penalty you have to pick through to get to the bit you really want to eat. So that's why I've called them 'squashed fly' muffins, to make them more fun!

1 Heat the oven to 190°C/375°F/gas 5. Line a 12-hole patty tin with paper cases.

2 Sift the flour and baking powder into a bowl and add the sugar and raisins and stir to combine.

3 Put the yogurt, egg and sunflower oil into a jug and mix together with a fork until smooth.

4 Stir the wet ingredients into the dry until just combined.

5 Spoon the mixture into the paper muffin cases and bake for 6–8 minutes until the muffins are well risen and firm.

MAKES 12 PATTY TIN SIZED MUFFINS / READY IN 30 MINUTES

150g | 5oz plain flour
5ml | 1 tsp baking powder
75g | 3oz golden caster sugar
50g | 2oz raisins
150 ml | 5fl oz your favourite flavoured yogurt
1 medium egg
60ml | 4 tbsp sunflower oil

Classic Combinations

Some of my favourite recipes are traditional ones. Although I enjoy experimenting with new ingredients and flavour combinations, I don't like adding new or unnecessary ingredients just for the sake of it. If you can make a perfectly good muffin with ten ingredients, why use 14? That's the approach I've taken with the recipes in this chapter – they're tried, tested and trusted family favourites. They're the sort of muffins that don't cost a fortune to make and would go down really well at a school bake sale.

Lemon and poppy seed muffins

Poppy seeds not only add an interesting texture to these muffins but also have added health benefits. Just 15ml/1 tbsp of poppy seeds a day gives you more than 10 per cent of your daily calcium requirement.

MAKES 12 / READY IN 30 MINUTES

100ml | 4fl oz sunflower oil
100g | 3½oz golden caster sugar
2 medium eggs
250ml | 9fl oz natural yogurt
Finely grated zest and juice of 2 lemons
75g | 3oz poppy seeds
300g | 11oz self-raising flour
2.5ml | ½ tsp bicarbonate of soda

1 Pre-heat the oven to 200°C/400°F/gas 6. Line a 12-hole muffin tin with paper muffin cases.
2 In a large jug mix together the sunflower oil, sugar, eggs, yogurt, lemon zest and juice and poppy seeds.
3 Put the flour and bicarbonate of soda into a bowl, pour on the wet ingredients but do not over mix.
4 Spoon the mixture into the paper muffin cases and bake for 15 minutes until well risen and firm.

Sticky ginger and golden syrup muffins

These moist muffins will keep for up to five days if stored in a cool place in a sealed container.

MAKES 12 / READY IN 25 MINUTES

200g | 7oz self-raising flour
2.5ml | ½ tsp bicarbonate of soda
5ml | 1 tsp mixed spice
15ml | 1 tbsp ground ginger
100ml | 4fl oz sunflower oil
100g | 3½oz golden syrup
100g | 3½oz dark muscovado sugar
2 medium eggs
200ml | 7fl oz milk

1 Pre-heat the oven to 200°C/400°F/gas 6. Line a 12-hole muffin tin with paper muffin cases.
2 Sieve the flour, bicarbonate of soda, mixed spice and ginger into a bowl.
3 In a jug mix together the oil, golden syrup, muscovado sugar, eggs and milk.
4 Pour the wet ingredients into the dry, then gently mix them together. Spoon the mixture into the muffin cases and bake for 10–15 minutes until well risen and firm.

Buttery vanilla muffins

With just a handful of ingredients in these muffins, you can really appreciate how good plain muffins are. These are best enjoyed on the day they are made, so why not bake half a dozen and freeze the remainder unbaked? They'll take 25 minutes to cook from frozen.

MAKES 12 / READY IN 30 MINUTES

75g | 3oz butter

200g | 7oz plain flour

2.5ml | ½ tsp bicarbonate of soda

10ml | 2 tsp baking powder

125g | 4oz golden caster sugar

1 large egg

284ml carton of soured cream

15ml | 1 tbsp vanilla extract

1 Pre-heat the oven to 200°C/400°F/gas 6. Line a 12-hole muffin tin with paper muffin cases.
2 Melt the butter in a bowl in the microwave for 50 seconds on high (850w), or in a pan.
3 Mix the flour, bicarbonate of soda, baking powder and sugar together in a bowl.
4 Mix together the egg, soured cream, melted butter and vanilla extract, then pour into the dry ingredients and stir.

5 Spoon the mixture into the muffin cases and bake for 15 minutes until pale golden, risen and firm.

Cook's tip: If you have about 100g | 3½oz of fruit you'd like to use up, try adding it, chopped, to the mixture with the flour. Well-drained tinned fruit works just as well as fresh. Try apricots, peaches, pineapple, mandarins, strawberries, rhubarb, raspberries, blackcurrants or cherries. Toss the fruit into the flour first to prevent it sinking during baking.

Apple and cinnamon crumble muffins

The pecan nuts, cinnamon and sugar give these an interesting crunchy crust.

MAKES 12 / READY IN 35 MINUTES

225g | 8oz plain flour

75g | 3oz golden caster sugar

10ml | 2 tsp baking powder

5ml | 1 tsp cinnamon

Pinch of salt

1 medium egg

150ml | 5fl oz semi-skimmed milk

2 apples, peeled, cored and finely chopped

50ml | 2fl oz sunflower oil

25g | 1oz pecan nuts

50g | 2oz light muscovado sugar

1 Pre-heat the oven to 190°C/375°F/gas 5. Line a 12-hole muffin tin with paper muffin cases.
2 Put the flour, caster sugar, baking powder, 2.5ml | ½ tsp cinnamon and salt into a bowl.
3 Add the egg, milk, apple and oil and stir for a few seconds until just combined.

4 Spoon the mixture into the paper muffin cases.
5 Put the pecan nuts into a processor and whiz to chop finely, add the muscovado sugar and the remaining cinnamon. Sprinkle over each muffin.
6 Bake for 15–20 minutes until well risen and firm. Serve warm.

Mincemeat and rum muffins

Try these as an easy alternative to mince pies. There's no need to limit them to Christmas-time only, as the mincemeat adds a lovely moistness to the muffins which also helps them keep fresh for several days in an airtight container.

MAKES 12 / READY IN 35 MINUTES

50g | 2oz butter

350g | 12oz plain flour

50g | 2oz golden caster sugar

10ml | 2 tsp baking powder

150 ml | 5fl oz apple juice

2 medium eggs

250g | 9oz fruit mincemeat

12 sugar cubes

45ml | 3 tbsp rum

1 Pre-heat the oven to 190°C/375°F/gas 5. Line a 12-hole muffin tin with paper muffin cases.
2 Melt the butter in a bowl in the microwave for 50 seconds on high (850w), or in a pan.
3 Combine the flour, caster sugar and baking powder in a bowl and mix well.
4 Pour the melted butter into a jug with the apple juice and eggs. Beat together well with a fork.

5 Stir the liquid ingredients into the dry mixture, then add the mincemeat and stir until just moistened. Spoon the mixture into muffin cases.
6 Put the sugar cubes into a shallow bowl. Pour over the rum to soak, then put one on top of each muffin.
7 Bake for 15–20 minutes until well risen and firm.

Cheese and chutney muffins

Who doesn't enjoy a ploughman's lunch? A large chunk of cheese served with pickle or chutney, bread and some salad leaves. So why not combine those old favourites in these scrumptious savoury muffins and serve them with some crunchy carrot and celery sticks – they're perfect for a packed lunch.

MAKES 12 / READY IN 40 MINUTES

50g | 2oz butter, plus extra for greasing

1 medium egg

250ml | 9fl oz milk

5ml | 1 tsp English or French mustard

45ml | 3 tbsp chutney or pickle

150g | 6oz mature Cheddar cheese, grated

15ml | 1 tbsp baking powder

300g | 11oz plain flour

1.25ml | ¼ tsp salt

1 Pre-heat the oven to 190°C/375°F/gas 5. Grease a 12-hole muffin tray with butter.
2 Melt the butter in a bowl in the microwave for 50 seconds on high (850w), or in a pan.
3 Put the butter, egg, milk, mustard and chutney into a large bowl and mix well.

4 Add the cheese, baking powder, flour and salt. Stir together until just mixed.
5 Spoon into muffin cases and bake for 15–20 minutes until well risen and firm.

Cappuccino and chocolate chip

The perfect treat to go with your morning cup of espresso, latte or cappuccino. If you like a stronger flavour, add an extra teaspoon of instant coffee to the muffin mixture. Use a decaffeinated variety if that's what you prefer.

1 Pre-heat the oven to 190°C/375°F/gas 5. Line a 12-hole muffin tin with paper muffin cases.
2 Melt the butter in a bowl in the microwave for 50 seconds on high (850w), or in a pan.
3 In a large bowl, stir together the flour, sugar, baking powder, salt, instant coffee and cinnamon.
4 In a jug stir together the milk, egg and melted butter, until blended.
5 Pour the wet ingredients into the dry. Stir in the chocolate chunks.
6 Spoon the mixture into the paper muffin cases and bake for 15–20 minutes until well risen and firm.
7 Dust the muffins with icing sugar and a sprinkling of grated chocolate, if liked.

MAKES 12 / READY IN 35 MINUTES

125g | 4oz butter

300g | 11oz plain flour

150g | 5oz golden caster sugar

12.5ml | 2½ tsp baking powder

2.5ml | ½ tsp salt

15ml | 1 tbsp instant espresso coffee powder

2.5ml | ½ tsp ground cinnamon

250ml | 9fl oz semi-skimmed milk, heated and cooled

1 medium egg, lightly beaten

100g | 3½oz dark chocolate, cut into mini chunks (whiz in a blender for speed)

2 tbsp icing sugar, sifted

25g | 1oz dark chocolate, grated

Banana and toffee muffins

These banana muffins are made extra special by the surprise toffee centres.

1 Heat the oven to 190°C/375°F/gas 5. Line a 12-hole muffin tin with paper muffin cases.
2 Melt the butter in a bowl in the microwave for 50 seconds on high (850w), or in a pan.
3 Sift the flour and bicarbonate of soda into a bowl. Add the sugar.
4 Mash the bananas with a fork and add to the bowl.
5 Crack the egg into a jug. Add the milk and melted butter and mix together with a fork.
6 Stir the wet ingredients into the dry and mix together until just combined.
7 Spoon half the mixture into the paper muffin cases, top with a fudge toffee, then spoon over the remaining muffin mixture.
8 Bake for 15 minutes until they are well risen and firm.

Cook's tip: Toss the toffees in flour before adding them to stop them sinking during baking.

MAKES 12 / READY IN 30 MINUTES

75g | 3oz butter

275g | 10oz self-raising flour

5ml | 1 tsp bicarbonate of soda

125g | 4oz light muscovado sugar

3 large, ripe bananas (about 450g | 1lb)

1 large egg

50ml | 2fl oz milk

12 fudge toffees

Carrot and cream cheese muffins

These muffins taste so good even without the cream cheese frosting, but it does provide a gorgeously gooey finishing touch.

1 Heat the oven to 200°C/400°F/gas 6. Line a 12-hole muffin tin with 8 paper muffin cases.
2 Sift the flour, bicarbonate of soda, cinnamon and nutmeg into a bowl.
3 Pour the oil into a jug, add the soured cream, sugar and eggs and beat with a fork until well blended.
4 Pour the wet ingredients into the dry, add the carrots and gently stir everything together to combine.
5 Spoon into the prepared muffin cases and bake for 15–20 minutes until well risen and firm. Leave to cool.
6 Mix together the butter and cream cheese until softened and combined. Stir in the icing sugar and vanilla extract and mix together. Spread over the top of the cooled muffins.

MAKES 8 / READY IN 35 MINUTES

225g | 8oz self-raising flour
5ml | 1 tsp bicarbonate of soda
5ml | 1 tsp ground cinnamon
2.5ml | ½ tsp ground nutmeg
150ml | 5fl oz sunflower oil
150ml | 5fl oz soured cream
225g | 8oz golden caster sugar
2 large eggs
125g | 4oz carrots, peeled and coarsely grated

For the frosting:
50g | 2oz butter
200g | 7oz cream cheese
50g | 2oz unrefined golden icing sugar
1.25ml | ¼ tsp vanilla extract

Chocolate brownie muffins

There's a seriously large quantity of chocolate in these brownie muffins and that's what gives them their wicked fudgey centres. Many chefs suggest using plain chocolate that contains more than 70 per cent cocoa solids, but although I love dark chocolate I think that would make these brownies too bitter. Use a plain chocolate that has about 50 per cent cocoa solids.

1 Pre-heat the oven to 190°C/375°F/gas 5. Line a 12-hole muffin tin with paper muffin cases.
2 Put the chocolate and butter into a bowl and microwave on medium (500w) for 2 minutes, stir, then microwave on high (850w) for a further 2 minutes, or until just melted. Alternatively, melt in a bowl over a pan of simmering water.
3 Sift the flour into a bowl and stir in the sugar.
4 Add the milk and eggs to the chocolate and mix together.
5 Pour the wet ingredients into the dry and stir together to combine.
6 Spoon into the paper muffin cases and bake for 20 minutes until risen and just firm.

MAKES 12 / READY IN 35 MINUTES

350g | 12oz plain chocolate, broken into pieces
175g | 6oz butter
100g | 3½oz self-raising flour
225g | 8oz golden caster sugar
45ml | 3 tbsp milk
3 medium eggs

Something Savoury

Think of these savoury muffins as little flavoured breads with a lovely texture. Fast and easy to make, they're so versatile that once you've mastered a few of these recipes (and been complimented for your innovative cooking), I'm sure you'll want to try more. They're great to serve as flavoursome nibbles to go with drinks – make them in mini-muffin tins instead of the regular size and you'll get 36 (just cook them for a slightly shorter time). Fab for buffet parties too, or try them as an accompaniment for vegetable soups and salads.

Spicy tex-mex muffins

Cornmeal is made from milled corn or maize and adds an interesting texture to these muffins. Try serving these with guacamole, salsa and salad with a soured cream dressing. These are best eaten within two days.

1 Pre-heat the oven to 190°C/375°F/gas 5. Lightly grease a 12-hole muffin tin by brushing with oil or line the tin with paper muffin cases.
2 Tip the cornmeal, flour, salt and baking powder into a large bowl.
3 In a jug, mix together the eggs, Tabasco, sunflower oil and soured cream. Add this to the flour mixture and stir quickly to just combine.

4 Add the sweetcorn, goat's cheese, chilli and coriander and gently fold through.
5 Spoon into the muffin cases and bake for 15–20 minutes until well risen and firm.

Cook's tip: Wear rubber gloves when you deseed and chop chillies to ensure you don't get spicy seeds stuck under your fingernails as these could then irritate skin or eyes.

MAKES 12 / READY IN 35 MINUTES

Oil to grease
100g | 3½oz cornmeal
75g | 3oz plain flour
Pinch of salt
15ml | 1 tbsp baking powder
2 large eggs
Dash of Tabasco sauce
100ml | 4fl oz sunflower oil
150ml | 5fl oz soured cream
100g | 3½oz sweetcorn
100g | 3½oz goat's cheese, crumbled
1 red or green chilli, deseeded and chopped
2 tbsp freshly chopped coriander leaves

Walnut, leek and bacon muffins

Try these with a crunchy salad – watercress, romaine lettuce, celery and apple with a mustard dressing would work well together.

1 Pre-heat the oven to 190°C/375°F/gas 5. Grease a 12-hole muffin tin.
2 Microwave the bacon on high (850w) for 3 minutes until cooked or dry fry.
3 Put the leeks into a bowl with 15g | ½oz of the butter and microwave on high (850w) for 3 minutes until softened, or cook in a pan over a gentle heat.
4 Melt the remaining butter in the microwave on high (850w) for 50 seconds, or melt in a pan. Put the eggs into a large jug with the butter and crème fraîche and mix together with a fork. Season with salt and freshly ground black pepper.

5 Put the walnuts in a processor and whiz to chop, then add the flour, paprika, baking powder and half of the cheese. Blend together.
6 Pour in the wet ingredients, bacon and leeks and blend for a few seconds until just combined.
7 Spoon the mixture into the prepared muffin tins and bake for 15 minutes. Sprinkle the rest of the cheese over the top of the muffins and bake for a further 5–10 minutes until well risen and firm.

MAKES 12 / READY IN 40 MINUTES

4 rashers smoked rindless streaky bacon, chopped
1 small leek, finely chopped
75g | 3oz butter
2 large eggs
150g | 5oz crème fraîche
Salt and freshly ground black pepper
100g | 3½oz walnuts
75g | 3oz plain flour
1.25ml | ¼ tsp paprika
5ml | 1 tsp baking powder
50g | 2oz Emmenthal cheese, grated

Mushroom and sunblush tomato muffins

These would taste good with an Italian antipasti selection, for example mixed olives, assorted cured meats such as salami and Parma ham, and a handful of wild rocket leaves dressed with balsamic vinegar.

1 Pre-heat the oven to 220°C/475°F/gas 7. Line a 12-hole muffin tin with paper muffin cases.

2 Sieve the flour into a large bowl and add the cornmeal, salt and baking powder. Add the tomatoes, mushrooms and cheese.

3 Mix together the eggs, milk and oil with a fork. Pour the wet ingredients onto the dry and gently stir together to combine.

4 Spoon the mixture into the muffin cases, dividing equally.

5 Bake for 15 minutes until the muffins are well risen and firm.

Cook's tip: If these muffins are for a special occasion, try using soaked and chopped porcini mushrooms instead of the fresh mushrooms. They will give an intense flavour and will retain their firmness after cooking.

MAKES 12 / READY IN 30 MINUTES

200g | 7oz plain flour

75g | 3oz fine cornmeal

5ml | 1 tsp salt

15ml | 1 tbsp baking powder

4 sunblush tomatoes, drained from oil and chopped

50g | 2oz baby button mushrooms, sliced

50g | 2oz Pecorino cheese, grated

3 medium eggs, lightly beaten

300ml | 10fl oz milk

60ml | 4 tbsp light olive oil

Roast pepper and mozzarella cheese muffins

Roast your own pepper if you have time or look out for roasted marinated peppers sold in jars – they have a wonderful sweet flavour.

1 Pre-heat the oven to 190°C/375°F/gas 5. Grease 9 holes of a muffin tin or line with paper muffin cases.

2 In a large bowl, combine the wholemeal flour, plain flour, polenta, sugar, baking powder and salt. Add the pepper and stir to mix evenly.

3 Pour the milk, eggs and the olive oil into a jug and whisk together with a fork. Pour into the flour mixture and stir with a large spatula just until moistened, using no more than 15–20 strokes. The batter will be lumpy.

4 Half-fill the muffin cases with the mixture and put a cube of mozzarella cheese and some basil in the centre. Cover with the remaining mixture until mounded just level with the top of the pan.

5 Bake for 20–25 minutes, or until well risen and firm. Serve them warm.

MAKES 9/ READY IN 1 HOUR

125g | 4oz wholemeal plain flour

125g | 4oz plain flour

50g | 2oz polenta

15ml | 1 tbsp golden caster sugar

15ml | 1 tbsp baking powder

Pinch of salt

2 roasted peppers, drained from oil and chopped

250ml | 7fl oz semi-skimmed milk

2 large eggs

60ml | 4 tbsp light olive oil

75g | 3oz mozzarella cheese, cubed

15ml | 1 tbsp fresh basil leaves, torn

Italian pizza muffins

This recipe was inspired by a classic salami, tomato, cheese and garlic pizza.

1 Pre-heat the oven to 190°C/375°F/gas 5. Line a 12-hole muffin tin with paper muffin cases.

2 Cut the pepperoni slices in half. Set aside 12 halves and chop the remainder. Repeat for the olives.

3 Mix together the flour, baking powder, oregano, paprika and most of the cheese in a large bowl. Add the diced pepperoni, olives, tomato and garlic.

4 Pour the milk, eggs and oil into a jug and mix together with a fork.

5 Add the wet ingredients to the dry ingredients, mixing until just combined.

6 Spoon the mixture into the muffin cases. Put a slice of pepperoni and an olive on top of each muffin and sprinkle with the remaining grated cheese. Bake for 15–20 minutes until well risen and firm.

MAKES 12 / READY IN 35 MINUTES

12 slices pepperoni

12 pitted olives

250g | 9oz plain white flour

15ml | 1 tbsp baking powder

5ml | 1 tsp freshly chopped oregano (dried will do)

1.25ml | ¼ tsp paprika

175g | 6oz mozzarella cheese, grated

1 tomato, finely chopped

1 clove of garlic, peeled and crushed

200ml | 7fl oz skimmed milk

2 medium eggs, beaten

60ml | 4 tbsp olive oil

Polenta and cheese muffins

Eat these on the day they're made or, better still, enjoy them warm. Perfect served with a steaming bowl of mushroom soup.

1 Pre-heat the oven to 220°C/475°F/gas 7. Line 9 holes of a muffin tin with paper muffin cases.

2 Sieve the flour into a large bowl and add the polenta, sugar, salt, baking powder and ground peppercorns. Add 25g/1oz of the cheese.

3 Mix together the eggs, milk and olive oil with a fork. Pour the wet ingredients onto the dry and gently stir together to combine.

4 Spoon the mixture into the muffin cases, dividing equally. Sprinkle over the rest of the cheese.

5 Bake for 15 minutes until the muffins are well risen and firm.

MAKES 9 / READY IN 30 MINUTES

150g | 6oz plain flour

150g | 6oz polenta

10ml | 2 tsp golden caster sugar

5ml | 1 tsp salt

15ml | 1 tbsp baking powder

10ml | 2 tsp coarsely ground black peppercorns

50g | 2oz Parmesan cheese, grated

2 medium eggs, lightly beaten

225ml | 8fl oz skimmed milk

60ml | 4 tbsp light olive oil

Feta and olive muffins

These are perfect served alongside a big crunchy bowl of Greek salad.

MAKES 12 / READY IN 40 MINUTES

175g | 6oz pitted black olives, sliced

3 medium eggs

100g | 3½oz feta cheese, crumbled

50g | 2oz Parmesan cheese, freshly grated

1 onion, peeled and chopped

75ml | 3fl oz light olive oil

300ml | 10fl oz semi-skimmed milk

275g | 10oz self-raising flour

15ml | 1 tbsp freshly chopped thyme

Salt and freshly ground black pepper

1 Pre-heat the oven to 200°C/400°F/gas 6. Grease a 12-hole muffin tin or line with paper muffin cases.

2 Put the olives, eggs, feta cheese, half the Parmesan cheese, onion, oil and milk into a large bowl and mix well together.

3 Stir in the flour and thyme and season with a pinch of salt and plenty of freshly ground black pepper. Mix until all the ingredients are well combined.

4 Spoon the muffin mixture into the prepared muffin tins and sprinkle over the remaining Parmesan cheese.

5 Bake for 25–30 minutes until well risen and firm.

Pesto muffins

Keep a jar of pesto in the fridge, then you can make these quickly if unexpected guests arrive. Great with roasted tomato soup or tomato and mozzarella salad. Add a handful of freshly chopped basil for a special occasion.

MAKES 9 / READY IN 40 MINUTES

50g | 2oz pine nuts

1 clove of garlic, peeled and crushed

75ml | 3fl oz light olive oil

2 eggs

90ml | 6 tbsp pesto

50g | 2oz Parmesan cheese

250ml | 9fl oz milk

150g | 5oz self-raising flour

75g | 3oz wholemeal flour

1 Pre-heat the oven to 200°C/400°F/gas 6. Line 9 holes of a muffin tin with paper muffin cases.

2 Tip the pine nuts on a baking tray and place in the oven for 5 minutes until they become golden brown.

3 Put the garlic, olive oil, eggs, pesto, Parmesan and milk into a large bowl. Stir everything together with a fork until well mixed.

4 Sift in the self-raising flour and wholemeal flour, then add the toasted pinenuts. Gently work this into the wet mix.

5 Spoon the mixture into the paper muffin cases and bake for 15 minutes until well risen and firm.

Prawn and peppadew muffins

Peppadews are one of those secret power-packed ingredients that's well worth seeking out. A South African favourite, they add a spicy yet piquant and sweet kick to dishes, yet are no way near as fierce as traditional chillies. They are sold pickled in jars, and you can choose from the hot or mild varieties.

MAKES 12 / READY IN 35 MINUTES

100g | 3½oz prawns
50g | 2oz mild peppadews, chopped
1 spring onion, trimmed and chopped
100g | 3½oz garlic and herb cheese
150ml | 5fl oz soured cream
1 medium egg
75ml | 3fl oz light olive oil
150ml | 5fl oz skimmed milk
225g | 8oz plain flour
15ml | 1 tbsp baking powder
15ml | 1 tbsp golden caster sugar
Pinch of salt

1 Pre-heat the oven to 190°C/375°F/gas 5. Line a 12-hole muffin tin with paper muffin cases.
2 Combine the prawns, peppadew, spring onions, cheese and soured cream in a bowl. Add the egg, oil and milk.
3 Stir in the flour, baking powder, sugar and salt and mix until just combined.
4 Spoon the mixture into the prepared muffin cases. Bake for 20 minutes until well risen and firm.

Cheese, sage and onion muffins

Use this basic recipe and vary the cheese to make the muffins taste different each time. Why not try one of the following; Emmenthal, Gruyère, Jarlsberg, Bavarian smoked, mature Cheddar, red Leicester, double Gloucester, Wensleydale, Stilton, dolcelatte or sage derby. This recipe is a great choice for diabetics.

MAKES 12 / READY IN 40 MINUTES

1 onion, peeled and chopped
60ml | 4 tbsp light olive oil
1 medium egg
150ml | 5fl oz semi-skimmed milk
225g | 8oz self-raising flour
Pinch of salt
30ml | 2 tbsp poppy seeds
100g | 3½oz hard cheese, grated
15ml | 1 tbsp freshly chopped sage

1 Pre-heat the oven to 230°C/450°F/gas 7. Line a 12-hole muffin tray with paper muffin cases.
2 Put the onion in a bowl with 15ml | 1 tbsp of olive oil and microwave on high (850w) for 2½ minutes until tender. Alternatively, soften in a pan over a gentle heat.
3 Pour the egg, milk and 30ml | 2 tbsp of olive oil into a jug and stir with a fork.
4 Sift the flour and salt into a bowl. Pour in the wet ingredients. Add the onion, half the poppy seeds, half the grated cheese and the sage leaves. Mix together to make a stiff mixture.
5 Divide the mixture between the paper cases and sprinkle with the remaining cheese and poppy seeds. Drizzle the rest of the olive oil over the top.
6 Bake for 15 minutes until well risen and firm.

Slimline Selection

I'm always wary of shop-bought products that are labelled '90% fat free'. What it doesn't tell you on the packet, at first glance, is that although it's virtually fat free, it's laden with sugar. Then there's the sugar-free product, which is full of artificial sweeteners and fat. So what about the muffins included in this chapter? If you're following a sensible balanced diet and reserve one muffin for your treat of the day, these should be a guilt-free treat you can enjoy to eat. It may help to refer to the nutritional values on page 94. Freeze the rest of the batch to keep them out of temptation's way, and simply microwave them one at a time.

Blueberry and oat muffins

The oats and blueberries in these muffins are considered 'super foods' by some nutritionists, capable of filling you up for longer and supplying longer-lasting energy.

1 Pre-heat the oven to 200°C/400°F/gas 6. Line a 12-hole muffin tin with 8 paper muffin cases.
2 Stir together flours, baking powder and bicarbonate of soda in a bowl. Stir in the sugar and most of the oats. Make a well in the centre of the mixture.
3 Combine the egg, yogurt, oil and vanilla extract in a jug. Add the egg mixture all at once to the flour mixture. Stir just until moistened (the batter should be lumpy). Fold the blueberries into the batter.
4 Spoon the batter into the prepared muffin cases, filling each three-quarters full.
5 Bake for 16–18 minutes or until risen, firm yet springy and a cocktail stick inserted into the centre comes out clean. Cool or serve warm.

MAKES 8 / READY IN 30 MINUTES
125g | 4oz wholemeal plain flour
75g | 3oz plain flour
15ml | 1 tbsp baking powder
2.5ml | ½ tsp bicarbonate of soda
150g | 5oz golden caster sugar
75g | 3oz rolled oats
1 medium egg
150ml | 5fl oz natural yogurt
50ml | 2fl oz sunflower oil
2.5ml | ½ tsp vanilla extract
75g | 3oz blueberries

Low-fat berry and apple muffins

Not only are these muffins virtually fat free, they're low in cholesterol and sugar too. If you're watching your weight, it's worth buying fructose because it's a natural product that's sweeter than sugar so you need less. It also has a lower glycemic index, so that you're less likely to experience the sugar highs and lows that make you feel hungry.

1 Pre-heat the oven to 200°C/400°F/gas 6. Line a 12-hole muffin tin with paper muffin cases.
2 Put the cooking apple into a bowl with 15ml/1tbsp of fructose and 30ml/2tbsp of water. Microwave on high (850w) for 2 minutes until the apple is tender. (Alternatively, cook in a pan for a few minutes.) Whiz with a hand blender until smooth. Leave to cool.
3 In a large bowl, sieve the flour, baking powder, bicarbonate of soda, cinnamon and nutmeg. Toss the berries in the rest of the fructose, then the bran, unwhisked egg whites and yogurt.
4 Spoon the mixture into the paper muffin cases, sprinkle with demerara sugar and bake for 20 minutes until pale golden.

MAKES 12 / READY IN 35 MINUTES
1 cooking apple (225g | 8oz), peeled, cored and chopped
60ml | 4 tbsp fructose
200g | 7oz plain flour
7.5ml | 1½ tsp baking powder
1.25ml | ¼ tsp bicarbonate of soda
3.75ml | ¾ tsp ground cinnamon
1.25ml | ¼ tsp ground nutmeg
125g | 4oz frozen berries (blackberries, raspberries, cherries or a mixture)
50g | 2oz bran
2 egg whites
250ml | 9fl oz natural low-fat yogurt
15ml | 1 tbsp demerara sugar

Low-fat yogurt and sour cherry

The perfect virtually fat-free recipe – no added butter or oil and egg-free too. This is a great recipe that you can vary slightly each time you make it. Try dried mango, papaya, apple, pear or other dried red berries, or even chopped fresh fruit. Add a pinch of cinnamon, nutmeg or mixed spice to vary the flavour even more.

1 Pre-heat the oven to 200°C/400°F/gas 6. Line a 12-hole muffin tin with paper muffin cases.
2 Sieve the flour, baking powder and bicarbonate of soda into a large bowl. Add the sugar and cherries and mix to combine.

3 Stir together the yogurt, milk and vanilla extract, then pour into the dry ingredients and stir together until just combined.
4 Spoon the mixture into the paper cases. Bake for 18 minutes until well risen and firm yet springy.

MAKES 12 / READY IN 30 MINUTES
225g | 8oz plain flour
10ml | 2 tsp baking powder
5ml | 1 tsp bicarbonate of soda
150g | 5oz golden caster sugar
25g | 1oz sour cherries
150ml | 5fl oz natural low-fat yogurt
150ml | 5fl oz skimmed milk
5ml | 1 tsp vanilla extract

Ricotta and spinach

Eat these flour and wheat-free muffins with a generous portion of green vegetables for a healthy, balanced meal. Super served warm or cold for a packed lunch or picnic as a great pastry-free alternative to quiche.

1 Pre-heat the oven to 180°C/350°F/gas 4. Grease a 12-hole muffin tin with butter.
2 Bake the pine nuts for 10 minutes until they are slightly browned.
3 Put the washed spinach into a bowl with 30ml | 2tbsp cold water, cover with cling film, pierce and microwave on high (850w) for 3 minutes until wilted. Alternatively, put the washed spinach in a pan and heat until just wilted. Tip into a sieve, squeeze out the excess water using a potato masher, then roughly chop.

4 In a jug mix together the ricotta, Parmesan, soured cream and eggs. Season with salt and freshly ground black pepper.
5 Stir in the spinach and toasted pine nuts.
6 Spoon into muffin tins and bake for 20 minutes or until a cocktail stick inserted into the centre comes out clean.

Cook's tip: Instead of ricotta, you can use a mixture of low-fat cream cheese and mild goats' cheese.

MAKES 12 / READY IN 35 MINUTES
Knob of butter
50g | 2oz pine nuts
225g | 8oz baby spinach leaves, washed
350g | 12oz ricotta
50g | 2oz Parmesan cheese, freshly grated
284ml carton soured cream
2 medium eggs
Salt and freshly ground black pepper

Cinnamon English muffins

These muffins are virtually sugar free, yet are still the business!

1 Sift the flour, cinnamon and salt into a bowl. Microwave on medium (500w) for 1 minute to warm slightly (this simply helps the yeast to act more quickly, so don't worry if you don't have a microwave).
2 Add the yeast and honey to the flour.
3 Pour the milk into a jug, add the butter and microwave on high (850w) for 1½ minutes to warm the milk and melt the butter. Alternatively, melt in a pan.
4 Stir all the liquid into the warm flour and beat well until smooth and elastic. Cover and prove in a warm place for 30 minutes or until doubled in bulk.
5 Turn onto a well-floured board and knead, working in a little more flour if necessary to make the dough easier to shape. Round up the dough, roll into a thick sausage shape and, using a sharp knife, slice into 10 portions, each about 3cm | 1¼ in thick.
6 Use a plain cutter to help shape each one into a round with straight sides. Place, well spaced out, on a greased baking sheet. Cover with greased cling film and put in a warm place to prove for 30–40 minutes or until springy to the touch.
7 Heat a griddle until really hot and grease lightly with butter. Lift the muffins carefully onto the hot griddle and cook a few at a time over very low heat for 8–10 minutes until pale gold underneath. Turn over and cook the other side.
8 Wrap in a cloth and keep warm if cooking in batches. To serve, insert a knife in the side, pull the top and bottom slightly apart, and insert slivers of butter.

MAKES 10 / READY IN 1 HOUR 25 MINUTES

450g | 1lb strong white bread flour
5ml | 1 tsp ground cinnamon
5ml | 1 tsp salt
7g sachet easy-blend dried yeast
5ml | 1 tsp runny honey
250ml | 9fl oz milk
50g | 2oz butter

Cook's tip: To save time, make and prove the dough in a bread machine, then shape and bake conventionally. Try serving toasted and topped with mashed banana.

Wholemeal yogurt and malted raisin

My favourite fat-free shop-bought treat is malt loaf. I've added malt extract to these muffins for a distinctive flavour – you'll find it sold in health food shops as it is a good source of vitamin B. Virtually fat free, these muffins make a guilt-free snack.

1 Pre-heat the oven to 200°C/400°F/gas 6. Line a 12-hole muffin tin with paper muffin cases.
2 Sieve the flour, cinnamon, mixed spice, baking powder and bicarbonate of soda into a large bowl with the salt. Add the wholemeal flour, sugar and raisins and mix.
3 Stir together the yogurt, malt extract and milk, then pour these into the dry ingredients and stir together until just combined.
4 Spoon the mixture into the paper cases. Bake for 18 minutes until risen, firm yet springy and a cocktail stick inserted into the centre comes out clean.

MAKES 12 / READY IN 30 MINUTES

100g | 3½oz plain flour
2.5ml | ½ tsp cinnamon
2.5ml | ½ tsp mixed spice
10ml | 2 tsp baking powder
5ml | 1 tsp bicarbonate of soda
Pinch of salt
125g | 4oz wholemeal flour
150g | 5oz golden caster sugar
25g | 1oz raisins
150ml | 5fl oz natural low-fat yogurt
15ml | 1 tbsp malt extract
150ml | 5fl oz skimmed milk

Butter-free chocolate and prune

What is the most common reaction to prunes? Err, no thanks. However, to my mind, the plump Californian ready-to-eat variety is an addictive snack. The other interesting discovery I made some years ago is that cooked and puréed prunes make a miraculous fat substitute. They keep the muffins moist and delicious, yet calorie controlled and cholesterol free. When combined with cocoa, no one will guess your secret ingredient!

MAKES 11 / READY IN 35 MINUTES

150g | 5oz plain flour
50g | 2oz cocoa powder
7.5ml | 1½ tsp baking powder
1.25ml | ¼ tsp bicarbonate of soda
1.25ml | ¼ tsp salt
200g | 7oz golden caster sugar
150g | 5oz pitted ready-to-eat prunes
3 large egg whites
5ml | 1 tsp vanilla extract

For the chocolate icing:
150g | 5oz icing sugar
15ml | 1 tbsp cocoa
15ml | 1 tbsp skimmed milk

1 Pre-heat the oven to 190°C/375°F/gas 5. Line 11 holes of a muffin tin with paper muffin cases.
2 Sieve the plain flour, cocoa, baking powder, bicarbonate of soda and salt into a bowl. Stir in the sugar.
3 Put the prunes into a food processor with 45ml | 3 tbsp of water and whiz to make a smooth purée. Add a further 250ml | 9fl oz of water, the egg whites and vanilla extract. Whiz again to combine.

4 Pour the wet ingredients into the dry ingredients and stir until well blended.
5 Spoon the mixture into the prepared muffin cases and bake for 8–10 minutes, until well risen and springy yet firm.
6 For the icing, sieve the icing sugar and cocoa together into a bowl, then stir in the milk until the icing is blended and smooth. Drizzle the icing over the cooled muffins to decorate.

Tangy cranberry

These are a welcome treat, and not oversweet. The cranberries add a zingy fruitiness.

MAKES 12 / READY IN 35 MINUTES

125g | 4oz fresh or frozen cranberries
25g | 1oz icing sugar
250g | 9oz plain flour
10ml | 2 tsp baking powder
150g | 5oz golden caster sugar
1 egg
250ml | 9fl oz milk
50g | 2oz unsalted butter, melted
icing sugar, sieved for dusting

1 Heat the oven to 200°C/400°F/gas 6. Line a 12-hole muffin tin with paper muffin cases.
2 Toss the cranberries in the icing sugar to coat. Sift the flour and baking powder into a large bowl. Stir in the caster sugar and cranberries.
3 In a large jug mix together the egg, milk and butter. Add the wet ingredients to the dry ingredients and gently stir everything together until just combined.

4 Spoon into the muffin cases and bake for 15 minutes until well risen and just firm.
5 Cool on a wire rack and dust with icing sugar to serve.

Cook's tip: Cranberries are only in season for a very short time. So stock up whilst they're in the shops and freeze for up to 6 months. Use straight from the freezer. Alternatively, use 100g | 3½oz of dried cranberries instead of the fresh; these are available all year. Omit the icing sugar.

Egg and bacon treats

Basically flour free, which makes them low in carbohydrates, these are quite unlike regular muffins in texture, but are still cooked in muffin tins for a defined shape. They would also be great for breakfast.

MAKES 9 / READY IN 35 MINUTES

Knob of butter

200g | 7oz rindless trimmed smoked back bacon, chopped

100g | 3½oz reduced fat mature Cheddar cheese, grated

284ml carton soured cream

4 medium eggs

Salt and freshly ground black pepper

1 Pre-heat the oven to 180°C/350°F/gas 4. Grease 9 holes of a muffin tin.
2 Dry fry the bacon for a few minutes until it is browned and becoming crispy. (Alternatively microwave on high (850w) for 4 minutes.)
3 In a jug use a fork to mix together the Cheddar cheese, soured cream and eggs. Season with salt and freshly ground black pepper. Stir in the bacon.
4 Spoon the mixture into the prepared muffin tins and bake for 20 minutes until firm.

Low-fat sultana bran English muffins

Why not make and shape these when you have time to spare, cook some straightaway and freeze the remainder unbaked?

MAKES 10 / READY IN 1 HOUR 25 MINUTES

225g | 8oz strong white bread flour

5ml | 1 tsp salt

225g | 8oz stoneground wholemeal flour

50g | 2oz bran

50g | 2oz sultanas

7g sachet easy-blend dried yeast

5ml | 1 tsp golden caster sugar

250ml | 9fl oz milk

25g | 1oz butter

1 Sift the white flour and salt into a bowl, then add the wholemeal flour. Microwave on medium (500w) for 1 minute, to warm slightly. This simply helps the yeast to act more quickly, so don't worry if you don't have a microwave.
2 Add the bran, sultanas, yeast and sugar to the bowl.
3 Pour the milk into a jug, add the butter and microwave on high (850w) for 1½ minutes to warm the milk and melt the butter. Alternatively, melt in a pan.
4 Stir all the liquid into the warm flour and beat well until smooth and elastic. Cover and prove in a warm place for 30 minutes or until doubled in bulk.
5 Turn onto a well-floured board and knead, working in a little more flour if necessary to make the dough easier to shape. Round up the dough, roll into a thick sausage shape and, using a sharp knife, slice into 10 portions, each about 3cm | 1¼in thick.
6 Use a plain cutter to help shape each one into a round with straight sides. Place, well spaced out, on a greased baking sheet. Cover with greased cling film and put in a warm place to prove for 30-40 minutes or until springy to the touch.
7 Heat a griddle until really hot and grease lightly with butter. Lift the muffins carefully onto the hot griddle and cook a few at a time over very low heat for 15 minutes until pale gold underneath. Turn over and cook the other side.
8 Wrap in a cloth and keep warm if cooking in batches. To serve, insert a knife in the side, pull the top and bottom slightly apart, and insert slivers of butter.

Cook's tip: If the outer edges of the muffins begin to burn before the centres are cooked, wrap the muffins in non-stick parchment paper and bake at 200°C/400°F/gas 6 for 5 minutes. (Frozen muffins are best baked in this way after griddling.)

Special Diets

Just because these recipes have been designed for people with special dietary needs doesn't mean they're going to be less tasty. Healthy muffins with less fat and sugar are no bad thing for any of us. If you're looking to expand your egg-free recipe repertoire, look for muffin recipes with just one egg, and replace it with 50ml/2fl oz milk. You'll be surprised how well it works. If you want to reduce your cholesterol, omit the butter and replace it with oil instead – use sunflower, vegetable, corn or light olive oil. If you can't eat foods containing gluten, try using gluten-free flour instead of regular flour. Also look out for gluten free baking powder or make your own substitute using 1 part bicarbonate of soda to 2 parts cream of tartar. For specific nutritional information on these recipes, please refer to page 94.

Cornmeal scones

These are not quite as light as regular scones, but they still taste really good, especially when served warm from the oven.

1 Pre-heat the oven to 220°C/425°F/gas 7. Place a baking sheet in the oven to heat up.
2 Put the cornmeal, gluten-free flour, baking powder, pinch of salt and butter into a food processor. Whiz the mixture for 30 seconds until it turns into crumbs. Tip the mixture into a bowl.
3 Add the sugar and buttermilk to the bowl. Use a knife to mix everything together.

4 Knead the dough lightly on a surface covered with baking parchment to make smooth dough.
5 Roll out the dough to about 2.5cm | 1in thickness. Dip a 6.5cm | 2½in plain cutter in flour and use it to stamp out 9 rounds of dough.
6 Use a palette knife to lift the scones onto the preheated baking sheet. Brush the tops with milk and bake for 12–15 minutes until the scones are risen and pale golden. Split and serve with butter or cream cheese.

GLUTEN-FREE, EGG-FREE

MAKES 9 / READY IN 30 MINUTES
150g | 5oz cornmeal
150g | 5oz gluten-free white flour
10ml | 2 tsp gluten-free baking powder
Pinch of salt
50g | 2oz butter, diced and chilled
25g | 1oz golden caster sugar
200ml | 7fl oz carton buttermilk
Milk, to glaze

Carrot and pineapple muffins

Moist and moreish, these muffins are egg and butter-free. For added fibre you could use wholemeal or granary flour.

1 Pre-heat the oven to 190°C/375°F/gas 5. Line a 12-hole muffin tin with paper muffin cases.
2 Beat together the sugar, oil and milk in a large bowl.
3 Sieve in the flour, bicarbonate of soda and cinnamon. Stir to moisten, then add the vanilla extract, carrots and pineapple.

4 Spoon the mixture into the prepared muffin cases and bake for 20 minutes until risen, firm yet springy and a cocktail stick inserted into the centre comes out clean.

Cook's tip: Add 50g | 2oz chopped nuts with the carrots for a little more crunch.

EGG-FREE

MAKES 12 / READY IN 35 MINUTES
225g | 8oz golden caster sugar
150ml | 5fl oz sunflower oil
150ml | 5fl oz semi-skimmed milk
225g | 8oz self-raising flour
5ml | 1 tsp bicarbonate of soda
5ml | 1 tsp cinnamon
5ml | 1 tsp vanilla extract
200g | 7oz carrots, finely grated
200g | 7oz canned crushed pineapple, drained

Buckwheat and apple muffins

Although buckwheat is actually a fruit seed related to rhubarb and sorrel, it behaves in a similar way to a cereal grain. For example, you can make buckwheat porridge. This makes it ideal for people who are sensitive to wheat or other grains that contain gluten. It adds an interesting texture to these muffins and gives a rich, dark brown colour.

1 Heat the oven to 190°C/375°F/gas 5. Line a 12-hole muffin tin with paper muffin cases.
2 Whisk together the honey, egg, oil, milk and vanilla.
3 In a bowl, combine the buckwheat flour, gluten-free flour, cinnamon and bicarbonate of soda. Add the apples, raisins and walnuts.
4 Stir the wet ingredients mixture into the apple mixture.
5 Spoon the mixture into the prepared muffin cases and bake for 15 minutes until pale golden, risen and firm.

GLUTEN-FREE

MAKES 12 / READY IN 35 MINUTES
- 225g | 8oz runny honey
- 1 large egg
- 75ml | 3fl oz sunflower oil
- 75ml | 3fl oz skimmed milk
- 5ml | 1 tsp vanilla extract
- 125g | 4oz buckwheat flour
- 125g | 4oz gluten-free white flour
- 5ml | 1 tsp cinnamon
- 10ml | 2 tsp bicarbonate of soda
- 2 eating apples, peeled, cored and chopped
- 200g | 7oz raisins
- 125g | 4oz walnuts, coarsely chopped

Gooseberry and almond muffins

Moist and fruity, these are lovely low-cholesterol muffins. When fresh gooseberries are not in season, use frozen. Cherries would work really well too, fresh when they're in season or drained, canned ones.

1 Heat the oven to 190°C/375°F/gas 5. Line a 12-hole muffin tin with paper muffin cases.
2 Mix together the sugar, olive oil, egg and milk and almond extract in a jug with a fork.
3 Sieve the flour and baking powder into a bowl, then add the ground almonds and mix together.
4 Toss in the gooseberries and coat in the flour. Mix in the wet ingredients and stir everything together until just combined.
5 Spoon the mixture into the prepared muffin cases. Sprinkle the muffins with the granulated sugar and flaked almonds and bake for 15–20 minutes until pale golden, well risen and firm.

GOOD FOR FIBRE

MAKES 12 / READY IN 35 MINUTES
- 175g | 6oz golden caster sugar
- 150 ml | 5fl oz light olive oil
- 1 medium egg
- 100ml | 4fl oz skimmed milk
- 5ml | 1 tsp almond extract
- 200g | 7oz self-raising flour
- 15ml | 1 tbsp baking powder
- 75g | 3oz ground almonds
- 200g | 7oz gooseberries, trimmed and halved
- 25g | 1oz golden granulated sugar
- 30ml | 2 tbsp flaked almonds

Sweet potato muffins

The sweet potatoes in this mix make the muffins lovely and moist.

1 Pierce the sweet potato several times, then microwave on high (850w) for 6 minutes. Alternatively, boil the sweet potato in its skin for 15–20 minutes until tender. Peel away the skin, put the flesh into a bowl and mash until smooth.

2 Heat the oven to 200°C/400°F/gas 6. Line 9 holes of a muffin tin with paper muffin cases.

3 Mix together the oil, sugar and eggs. Add the sweet potato, raisins and walnuts and stir well.

4 Sieve in the flour, baking powder and ground mixed spice, and mix just enough to moisten. Do not over-mix.

5 Spoon the mixture into the prepared muffin cases, sprinkle with the spice sugar mix and bake for 20 minutes until pale golden, well risen and firm.

MILK AND LACTOSE FREE

MAKES 9 / READY IN 35 MINUTES

225g | 8oz sweet potato, washed

75ml | 3fl oz sunflower oil

100g | 3½oz golden caster sugar

2 medium eggs

50g | 2oz raisins

50g | 2oz walnuts, chopped

175g | 6oz plain flour

10ml | 2 tsp baking powder

5ml | 1 tsp ground mixed spice

45ml | 3 tbsp golden granulated sugar mixed with 2.5ml | ½ tsp ground mixed spice, for sprinkling

Bran, date and prune muffins

These muffins are wholesome, satisfying and high in fibre. Why not bake six, then keep the rest of the mixture in the fridge overnight – this allows the bran to swell and makes the muffins taste even more scrumptious.

1 Put the flour, bicarbonate of soda, baking powder, mixed spice, sugar, bran, dates and prunes into a bowl.

2 In a jug, combine the sunflower oil, buttermilk and egg and mix until well blended.

3 Pour the wet ingredients into the dry, mix until just combined, cover and chill some of the mixture overnight if you like.

4 Heat the oven to 190°C/375°F/gas 5. Line a 12-hole muffin tin with paper muffin cases.

5 Spoon the mixture into the prepared muffin cases and bake for 20 minutes until pale golden, well risen and firm.

HIGH FIBRE

MAKES 12 / READY IN 35 MINUTES

150g | 6oz malted grain flour

10ml | 2 tsp bicarbonate of soda

2 tsp baking powder

2.5ml | ½ tsp ground mixed spice

125g | 4oz light muscovado sugar

50g | 2oz oat bran

100g | 3½oz dried pitted dates, chopped

100g | 3½oz ready-to-eat pitted prunes, chopped

100ml | 4fl oz sunflower oil

300ml | 10fl oz buttermilk

1 medium egg

Oatmeal and raspberry muffins

Oats and olive oil are good foods to eat if you are trying to reduce your cholesterol level. Using wholemeal flour instead of plain white flour would be even more healthy, or use a mixture of the two.

LOW IN SATURATED FAT

MAKES 12 / READY IN 35 MINUTES

100g | 3½oz rolled oats
250ml | 9fl oz skimmed milk
1 medium egg
200g | 7oz golden caster sugar
50ml | 2fl oz light olive oil
150g | 5oz plain flour
10ml | 2 tsp baking powder
2.5ml | ½ tsp bicarbonate of soda
100g | 3½oz raspberries
30ml | 2 tbsp rolled oats, to sprinkle

1 Pre-heat the oven to 190°C/375°F/gas 5. Line a 12-hole muffin tin with paper cases.
2 Put the oats into a bowl and add the milk.
3 In a jug mix together the egg, sugar and olive oil to combine.
4 Sieve the flour, baking powder and bicarbonate of soda into a bowl, then gently toss in the raspberries.
5 Gently stir in the egg mixture, then the oats and milk.

6 Spoon the mixture into the muffin cases and sprinkle over the rolled oats. Bake for 15-20 minutes until well risen and firm.

Cook's tip: Add 2.5ml | ½ tsp of cinnamon for added flavour. It's fine to use raspberries straight from the freezer, as this will help them to keep their shape rather than becoming squashed during mixing. Chopped dried apples, apricots, blueberries, cherries, dates, pears, raisins or sultanas also taste good.

Lactose-free courgette muffins

These have an interesting and mildly sweet flavour, so give them a try. We're all used to carrot cake, so why not courgettes?

LACTOSE-FREE

MAKES 12 / READY IN 35 MINUTES

3 medium eggs
100ml | 4fl oz sunflower oil
75ml | 3fl oz water
250g | 9oz golden caster sugar
350g | 12oz courgettes (zucchini), grated
10ml | 2 tsp baking powder
5ml | 1 tsp ground cinnamon
5ml | 1 tsp nutmeg
225g | 8oz plain flour
125g | 4oz raisins

1 Pre-heat the oven to 190°C/375°F/gas 5. Line a 12-hole muffin tin with paper muffin cases.
2 Mix together the eggs, sunflower oil, water, sugar and courgettes in a large bowl.
3 Add the baking powder, cinnamon, nutmeg, plain flour and raisins and blend until just mixed.

4 Spoon the mixture into the prepared muffin cases and bake for 15-20 minutes until pale golden, well risen and firm yet springy.

Cook's tip: For chocolate muffins, replace 25g | 1oz of the plain flour with cocoa powder. (These taste even better.)

Herb Popovers

Similar to English Yorkshire puddings, but you can start cooking these in a cold oven unlike the Yorkshire puds, which always need a sizzling hot oven to start.

1 Put the flour, salt and herbs into a bowl. Butter 6 holes of a mega-muffin tin.
2 In a jug mix the eggs and milk together very well with a fork.
3 Pour the wet ingredients into the dry and mix together with a fork until lump-free. Pour the batter into the buttered muffin tin.
4 Turn on the oven to 220°C/425°F/gas 7. Put the popoves into a cold oven.
5 Cook for 25-30 minutes. For drier popovers pierce each one with a knife and cook for 5 more minutes.

LOW-CARB

MAKES 6 MEGA-MUFFINS / READY IN 30-40 MINUTES

100g | 3½oz plain flour

¼ tsp salt

30ml | 2 tbsp freshly chopped herbs (such as chives, parsley, thyme, sage, basil or a mixture)

3 eggs

250ml | 8fl oz semi-skimmed milk

Sugar-free double-corn muffins

These muffins are ideal for diabetics and make a perfect replacement for bread. They're best eaten within two days of making. Freeze extras and defrost in the microwave until they are just warm to serve.

1 Pre-heat the oven to 200°C/400°/gas 6. Line 9 holes of a muffin tin with paper muffin cases.
2 Put the cornmeal, flour, baking powder and salt into a mixing bowl.
3 Add the sweetcorn, egg, oil and buttermilk, stirring well.
4 Spoon the mixture into the prepared muffin cases and bake for 20 minutes until pale golden, well risen and firm.

SUGAR-FREE

MAKES 9 / READY IN 35 MINUTES

100g | 3½oz cornmeal

125g | 4 oz plain flour

15ml | 1 tbsp baking powder

1.25ml | ¼ tsp salt

200g | 7oz sweetcorn

1 egg, lightly beaten

75ml | 3fl oz sunflower oil

284ml carton of buttermilk

Scones

Do you remember being taught how to make English scones at school? I do, and I think that's what may have put me off making them for ages. My memories are of rock-hard, tasteless mini-bricks. Maybe I didn't eat them the day they were made, or maybe I was too scared to add enough liquid to the dough to make it pliable. Well, put all those memories aside and follow these foolproof recipes. Home-made scones are soft, light and especially gorgeous eaten within a few hours of baking. They're the perfect accompaniment to a steaming cup of tea. Freezing the unbaked dough is a great option – just cook from the freezer for an extra 3 minutes.

English afternoon tea scones

These traditional scones are divine served with the updated alternative to clotted cream – mascarpone cream and jam.

1 Pre-heat the oven to 230°C/450°F/gas 8. Place an ungreased baking sheet in the oven to heat up.

2 Sift the flour, baking powder and salt together into a bowl and add the sugar.

3 Add the butter and rub together with your fingertips to make crumbs.

4 Pour in the egg and milk and bring the mixture together with your hands to make a soft manageable dough. Roll out dough on a lightly floured surface until it is 2cm | 3/4in thick. Use a 5cm | 2in plain cutter to stamp out 8 rounds.

5 Use a palette knife to lift the scones onto the pre-heated baking sheet. Brush the tops with milk.

6 Bake for 8–10 minutes until well risen, firm and golden. Cool on a wire rack.

7 Mix together the mascarpone, Greek yogurt, sugar and vanilla until well combined. Split scones in half and serve with a dollop of mascarpone and jam.

Cook's tip: You can still make these scones even if you have run out of eggs by using 150ml | 5fl oz milk or even a mixture of water and milk. They'll be slightly less rich, but tasty all the same.

MAKES 8 / READY IN 30 MINUTES

225g | 8oz self-raising flour
5ml | 1 tsp baking powder
Pinch of salt
30ml | 2 tbsp golden caster sugar
50g | 2oz butter, cubed
1 medium egg, lightly beaten
75ml | 3fl oz milk, plus a little extra to glaze

For the filling:
100g | 3 1/2oz mascarpone cheese
60ml | 4 tbsp Greek yogurt
30ml | 2 tbsp golden caster sugar
2.5ml | 1/2 tsp vanilla extract
120ml | 8 tbsp strawberry jam

Malted grain scones

I find that wholemeal goodies become addictive, the more you eat, the more you enjoy them. So here's a satisfying granary-style treat with an interesting texture. It's tasty cut in half and spread with butter and jam.

MAKES 8 / READY IN 30 MINUTES

225g | 8oz malted grain flour

15ml | 1 tbsp baking powder

Pinch of salt

15ml | 1 tbsp golden caster sugar

50g | 2oz butter, cubed

150ml | 5fl oz skimmed milk, plus a little extra to glaze

1 Pre-heat the oven to 230°C/450°F/gas 8. Place an ungreased baking sheet in the oven to heat up.

2 Tip the flour, baking powder and salt into a bowl and add the sugar.

3 Add the butter and rub together with your fingertips to make crumbs.

4 Pour in the milk and bring the mixture together with your hands to make a soft, manageable dough. Roll out dough on a lightly floured surface until it is 2cm | ³/₄in thick. Use a 5cm | 2in plain cutter to stamp out 8 rounds.

5 Use a palette knife to lift the scones onto the pre-heated baking sheet. Brush the tops with milk.

6 Bake for 8–10 minutes until well risen, firm and golden.

Sunflower seed and honey scones

Sunflower seeds are a brilliant source of vitamin E, and folic acid, other B vitamins, and minerals including copper and magnesium. The seeds add an interesting crunchiness to the scones.

MAKES 8 / READY IN 30 MINUTES

125g | 4oz white self-raising flour

Pinch of salt

5ml | 1 tsp baking powder

100g | 3¹/₂oz wholemeal self-raising flour

50g | 2oz sunflower seeds

50g | 2oz butter, cubed

1 egg, lightly beaten

75ml | 3fl oz milk, plus a little extra to glaze

30ml | 2 tbsp runny honey

1 Pre-heat the oven to 230°C/450°F/gas 8. Place an ungreased baking sheet in the oven to heat up.

2 Sift the white flour, salt and baking powder together into a bowl, then add the wholemeal flour and half of the seeds.

3 Add the butter and rub together with your fingertips to make crumbs.

4 Pour in the egg, milk and honey and bring the mixture together with your hands to make it a soft, manageable dough. Roll out dough on a lightly floured surface until it is 2cm | ³/₄in thick. Use a 5cm | 2in fluted cutter to stamp out 8 rounds.

5 Use a palette knife to lift the scones onto the pre-heated baking sheet. Brush the tops with milk and sprinkle with the rest of the sunflower seeds.

6 Bake for 8–10 minutes until well risen, firm and golden. Cool on a wire rack, then serve split and buttered, with extra thick honey.

Cheddar and thyme scones

Serve these scones with cheese, chutney and celery sticks at lunchtime to make a change from bread.

MAKES 8 / READY IN 30 MINUTES

225g | 8oz self-raising flour
Pinch of salt
5ml | 1 tsp baking powder
40g | 1½oz butter, cubed
75g | 3oz mature Cheddar cheese, grated
2 sprigs of thyme
5ml | 1 tsp whole grain mustard
150 ml | 5fl oz milk, plus a little extra to glaze

1 Pre-heat the oven to 220°C/425°F/gas 7. Place an ungreased baking sheet in the oven to heat up.
2 Sieve the flour, salt and baking powder into a bowl and rub in the butter, until the mixture forms into crumbs.
3 Stir in half the cheese. Strip the thyme leaves off the stalks and add the leaves along with the mustard and enough milk to give a fairly soft dough.
4 Roll out dough on a lightly floured surface until it is 2cm | ¾in thick. Use a 5cm | 2in plain cutter to stamp out 8 rounds.
5 Use a palette knife to lift the scones onto the baking sheet. Brush the tops with milk and sprinkle with the rest of the cheese.
6 Bake for 8–10 minutes until well risen, firm and golden.

Carrot and raisin scones

This is an interesting combination that's not over-sweet. I recommend them spread with cream cheese.

MAKES 8 / READY IN 30 MINUTES

250g | 9oz self-raising flour, sifted
5ml | 1 tsp baking powder
Pinch of salt
50g | 2oz butter, diced and chilled
25g | 1oz golden caster sugar
50g | 2oz raisins
75g | 3oz carrots, grated
250ml | 9fl oz buttermilk
Milk, to glaze

1 Pre-heat the oven to 220°C/425°F/gas 7. Place an ungreased baking sheet in the oven to heat up.
2 Put the flour, baking powder, salt and butter in a food processor. Whiz the mixture for 30 seconds until the mixture turns into crumbs. Tip the mixture into a bowl.
3 Add the sugar, raisins, carrots and buttermilk. Use a knife to mix everything together.
4 Knead the dough lightly on a floured surface to make a smooth dough. Roll out the dough to a thickness of about 2.5cm | 1in.
5 Dip a 6.5cm | 2½in plain cutter in some flour, then use it to stamp out 8 rounds of dough.
6 Use a palette knife to lift the scones onto the pre-heated baking sheet. Brush the tops with milk and bake for 12–15 minutes until the scones are risen and pale golden.

Wholemeal scone round

Although these are called wholemeal scones, they do contain some white flour to guarantee that they are light. Using brown flour on its own would make the texture of the scone too dense.

1 Pre-heat the oven to 220°C/425°F/gas 7. Place an ungreased baking sheet in the oven to heat up.
2 Sift the white flour, salt and baking powder together into a bowl. Tip in the wholemeal flour and sugar.
3 Add the butter and rub together with your fingertips to make crumbs.
4 Pour in the milk and bring the mixture together with your hands to make it a soft, manageable dough.

5 Shape into a flat 15cm | 6in round. Mark into 6 triangular slices using the back of floured knife.
6 Put the scone onto the pre-heated baking sheet and bake at once for 15 minutes until pale golden. To test if it is cooked, tap the base with your knuckle – it should sound hollow.

SERVES 6 / READY IN 30 MINUTES
50g | 2oz plain white flour
Pinch of salt
15ml | 1 tbsp baking powder
175g | 6oz plain wholemeal flour
50g | 2oz golden caster sugar
50g | 2oz butter, cubed
150ml | 5fl oz milk

Vanilla and buttermilk scones

The more expensive your vanilla flavouring, the more pungent the flavour will be. Vanilla essence is an artificial flavouring that's best avoided. Splash out on the real thing – vanilla extract – and you'll appreciate its distinctive flavour. Yet more indulgent is vanilla bean paste. It is a fantastic ingredient, expensive but a little goes a long way. It's thicker than vanilla extract and contains millions of the tiny vanilla seeds you find when you split a vanilla pod.

1 Pre-heat the oven to 220°C/425°F/gas 7. Place an ungreased baking sheet in the oven to heat up.
2 Tip the flour, baking powder, salt and butter in a food processor. Whiz the mixture for 30 seconds until the mixture turns into crumbs. Tip the mixture into a bowl.
3 Add the sugar, buttermilk and vanilla bean paste or extract. Use a knife to mix everything together.

4 Knead the dough lightly on a floured surface to make a smooth dough. Roll out the dough to a thickness of about 2.5cm | 1in.
5 Dip a 6.5cm | 2½in plain cutter in some flour, then use it to stamp out 8 rounds of dough.
6 Use a palette knife to lift the scones onto the preheated baking sheet. Brush the tops with milk and bake for 12–15 minutes until the scones are risen and pale golden. Split and serve with jam.

MAKES 8 / READY IN 30 MINUTES
250g | 9oz self-raising flour, sifted
5ml | 1 tsp baking powder
Pinch of salt
50g | 2oz butter, diced and chilled
25g | 1oz golden caster sugar
250ml | 9fl oz buttermilk
5ml | 1 tsp vanilla bean paste or vanilla extract
Milk, to glaze

Buttermilk drop scones

So speedy to make - the perfect thing to make for a comforting dessert or afternoon treat.

1 Sieve the flour, baking powder and salt into a bowl. Make a well in the centre.
2 Mix together the eggs, buttermilk and 3 tbsp cold water, then pour the wet ingredients into the dry and whisk everything together to make a smooth batter.
3 Heat the oil in a large, heavy-based pan. Add 3 separate ladlefuls of the mixture to the hot pan. Cook for 2-3 minutes until the bases are firm, then use a spatula to turn the pancakes over. Cook for a further 2-3 minutes until the pancakes are spongy and cooked through.

4 Put the blueberries and sugar into a pan with 100ml | 4fl oz water. Bring to the boil and simmer for a few minutes. Mix the arrowroot with 1 tbsp cold water to make a smooth paste, then add to the pan. Stir over the heat until thickened and smooth.
5 Serve 2-3 pancakes layered up and drizzled with the blueberries in syrup.

Cooks tip: These taste just as good drizzled with maple syrup and sliced bananas. Or try them sprinkled with golden caster sugar and a squeeze of lemon.

MAKES 6 / READY IN 15 MINUTES

150g | 6oz plain flour
½ tsp baking powder
pinch of salt
3 large eggs
150ml | 5fl oz buttermilk
2 tbsp sunflower oil

To serve:
150g | 6oz blueberries
50g | 2oz golden caster sugar
1 tsp arrowroot

Blueberry and cinnamon scones

Dried blueberries make a welcome change from more common dried fruit, such as sultanas, and the hint of cinnamon is lovely. Split and spread with a little butter is all you need.

MAKES 8 / READY IN 30 MINUTES

250g | 9oz self-raising flour, sifted
5ml | 1 tsp baking powder
2.5ml | ½ tsp cinnamon
Pinch of salt
50g | 2oz butter, diced and chilled
25g | 1oz golden caster sugar
250ml | 9fl oz buttermilk
50g | 2oz dried blueberries
Milk to glaze

1 Pre-heat the oven to 220°C/425°F/gas 7. Place an ungreased baking sheet in the oven to heat up.
2 Tip the flour, baking powder, cinnamon, salt and butter in a food processor. Whiz the mixture for 30 seconds until it turns into crumbs. Tip the mixture into a bowl.
3 Add the sugar, buttermilk and blueberries. Use a knife to mix everything together.
4 Knead the dough lightly on a floured surface to make a smooth dough. Roll out to a thickness of about 2.5cm | 1 in.
5 Dip a 6.5cm | 2½in plain cutter in some flour, then use it to stamp out 8 rounds of dough.
6 Use a palette knife to lift the scones onto the pre-heated baking sheet. Brush the tops with milk and bake for 12–15 minutes until the scones are risen and pale golden.

Cranberry and walnut scones

These scones are a great combination of ingredients. They are at their best when split and served with blueberry jam.

MAKES 8 / READY IN 30 MINUTES

50g | 2oz walnuts
250g | 9oz self-raising flour, sifted
50g | 2oz self-raising wholemeal flour
5ml | 1 tsp baking powder
Pinch of salt
50g | 2oz butter, diced and chilled
25g | 1oz golden caster sugar
50g | 2oz dried cranberries
250ml | 9fl oz buttermilk
Milk, to glaze

1 Pre-heat the oven to 220°C/425°F/gas 7. Place an ungreased baking sheet in the oven to heat up.
2 Put the walnuts into a processor and whiz until finely ground.
3 Add the flours, baking powder, salt and butter to the food processor. Whiz the mixture for 30 seconds until it turns into crumbs. Tip the mixture into a bowl.
4 Add the sugar, cranberries and buttermilk. Use a knife to mix everything together.
5 Knead the dough lightly on a floured surface to make a smooth dough. Roll out to a thickness of about 2.5cm | 1in.
6 Dip a 6.5cm | 2½in plain cutter in some flour, then use it to stamp out 8 rounds of dough.
7 Use a palette knife to lift the scones onto the pre-heated baking sheet. Brush the tops with milk and bake for 12–15 minutes until the scones are risen and pale golden. Split and serve with jam.

Time to Indulge

I've a confession to make. The only reason I really started cooking was because I'm greedy. If I had a chocolate craving, the fastest and most efficient way of getting that satisfying hit was to whip something up in the kitchen. If I was feeling lazy, I may have munched on raisins or a banana, tried coffee with frothy milk and an extra-large sprinkling of chocolate, but by the time I'd waded through all those nibbles, I hadn't fully satisfied the craving and I'd still consumed a fair few calories. So, for those times when only the biggest and best will do, here are ten totally wicked muffins.

Stem ginger muffins

I adore ginger – the stronger the flavour, the better it is for me. Look out for crystallized ginger that has a fantastically powerful ginger hit – it's great to use for decorating cakes and muffins. Stem ginger in syrup never fails to please either. These muffins will keep for up to a week, stored in a cool place in an airtight container.

1 Heat the oven to 180°C/350°F/gas 4. Line a 6-hole mega-muffin tin with paper muffin cases.
2 Put the butter, sugar and black treacle into a jug and microwave on high (850w) for 2 minutes until everything has melted together. Alternatively, heat gently in a pan, then pour into a jug.
3 Add the milk and Southern Comfort, if using, to the jug and mix together. Stir in the egg.
4 Sift the flour, spices and bicarbonate of soda into a large mixing bowl. Stir in the stem ginger and apricots to coat.

5 Make a well in the centre and pour in the wet ingredients. Stir gently until everything is combined.
6 Spoon the mixture into the muffin cases and bake for 20–25 minutes, until well risen and firm.

Cook's tip: Once a packet of muscovado sugar has been opened, it quickly goes hard. Make it spoonable again by microwaving on defrost (150w) for 30 seconds for about 225g | 8oz.

MAKES 6 MEGA-MUFFINS / READY IN 40 MINUTES

100g | 3½oz butter
100g | 4oz light muscovado sugar
45ml | 3 tbsp black treacle
100ml | 3½fl oz skimmed milk
30ml | 2 tbsp Southern Comfort, optional
1 large egg
150g | 5oz plain flour
15ml | 1 tbsp ground ginger
10ml | 2 tsp ground cinnamon
5ml | 1 tsp bicarbonate of soda
6 stem ginger, drained from syrup and roughly chopped
75g | 3oz dried apricots, chopped

Strawberries and cream

If you have bought strawberries that have gone mushy sooner than expected, put them to good use in these divine dessert muffins. Serve them topped with whole strawberries and fresh vanilla cream.

1 Heat the oven to 200°C/400°F/gas 6. Line a 6-hole mega-muffin tin with paper muffin cases.
2 Sift the flour and baking powder into a bowl. Add the sugar and gently stir in the strawberries, to coat.
3 In a jug mix the eggs, oil, milk and vanilla extract. Beat until well blended.
4 Add the egg mixture to the flour mixture and stir for just 10–15 strokes to combine.

5 Spoon the mixture into the paper cases. Bake for 20 minutes until well risen and firm. Cool on a wire rack.
6 Whip the cream with the sugar and vanilla extract until just standing in soft peaks. Put a dollop of cream on top of each muffin and serve with a fresh strawberry.

MAKES 6 MEGA-MUFFINS / READY IN 30 MINUTES

300g | 11oz plain flour
10ml | 2 tsp baking powder
175g | 6oz golden caster sugar
125g | 4oz strawberries, chopped
3 medium eggs
75ml | 3fl oz sunflower oil
100ml | 4fl oz skimmed milk
5ml | 1 tsp vanilla extract

To serve:
150ml | 5fl oz double cream
15ml | 1 tbsp golden caster sugar
2.5ml | ½ tsp vanilla extract
6 whole strawberries

Mixed nut and muscovado muffins

The rich, dark colour of these egg-free muffins comes from using dark muscovado sugar, which also gives them a wonderfully treacly taste. Great eaten straight from the oven, but also good enjoyed one or two days later when the moisture in the sugar softens the muffins.

MAKES 4 MEGA-MUFFINS / READY IN 35 MINUTES

75g | 3oz wholemeal plain flour

175g | 6oz plain flour

75g | 3oz dark muscovado sugar

15ml | 1 tbsp baking powder

1.25ml | ¼ tsp bicarbonate of soda

125g | 4oz mixed nuts, such as pecans, macadamias and hazelnuts, chopped

60ml | 4 tbsp golden syrup

75ml | 3fl oz sunflower oil

150ml | 5fl oz skimmed milk

1 Heat the oven to 190°C/375°F/gas 5. Line 4 holes of a mega-muffin tin with paper muffin cases.

2 Put the wholemeal flour, plain flour, sugar, baking powder, bicarbonate of soda and most of the nuts in a large bowl and mix well.

3 Pour 90ml | 6 tbsp boiling water into a jug, dip a tablespoon (the measuring spoon type) into the hot water and use to measure out the golden syrup, add to the water with the oil and milk.

4 Quickly mix the wet ingredients into the dry and spoon the mixture into the muffin cases. Sprinkle over the reserved nuts.

5 Bake for about 20-25 minutes until risen, just firm to the touch and a cocktail stick inserted into the centre comes out clean.

Coconut, carrot, pecan and pineapple muffins

These are the kind of muffins that would be labelled 'healthy' in the shops, just because they've got carrots in the ingredients list. This is really the greedy version of a good-for-you muffin, but each one contains a fruit and vegetable so they're certainly not all bad.

MAKES 6 MEGA-MUFFINS / READY IN 60 MINUTES

225g | 8oz plain flour

5ml | 1 tsp ground cinnamon

5ml | 1tsp mixed spice

15ml | 1 tbsp baking powder

2.5ml | ¼ tsp salt

225g | 8oz golden caster sugar

250g | 9oz carrots, peeled and grated

1 apple, peeled, cored and grated

50g | 2oz sweetened and tenderised shredded coconut

100g | 3½oz raisins

75g | 3oz pecans or walnuts, roughly chopped

125g | 4oz crushed pineapple, drained from can

2 medium eggs

150ml | 5fl oz vegetable oil

150ml | 5fl oz soured cream

5ml | 1 tsp vanilla extract

1 Heat the oven to 190°C/375°F/gas 5. Line a 6-hole mega-muffin tin with paper muffin cases.

2 Sift together the flour, cinnamon, mixed spice, baking powder and salt. Stir in the sugar, carrots, apple, coconut, raisins, nuts and pineapple.

3 In a jug, whisk together the eggs, oil, soured cream and vanilla extract. Pour into the bowl with the dry ingredients and stir together until just combined.

4 Spoon the batter into the paper cases, filling them almost to the top. Bake for 25-30 minutes until risen, firm and springy or until a cocktail stick inserted into the centre comes out clean.

5 Cool the muffins in the tin for about 10 minutes, then turn out onto a wire rack to cool completely. Store in an airtight container. Best eaten the next day, if you can wait.

Sticky toffee and date muffins

As these muffins come with a sticky toffee sauce, serve them warm as a gorgeous pud.

1 Heat the oven to 180°C/350°F/gas 4. Grease 8 holes in a mega-muffin tin.
2 Put the dates into a large jug and add the bicarbonate of soda and the butter. Pour over 250ml | 9fl oz boiling water and leave for a few minutes to cool slightly. Then whiz to a smooth purée in a processor.
3 Sift the flour and baking powder into a large bowl, add the sugar, eggs and date purée and stir until just combined.
4 Spoon into the prepared muffin tins and bake for 25 minutes until risen, firm and springy.

5 Meanwhile, for the sauce, put the butter, sugar and 100ml/4floz of the cream into a large jug. Microwave on high (850w) for 2 minutes, stir and cook for another 2 minutes until the sauce is melted and smooth. Alternatively, heat in a pan and stir until melted.
6 Whip the remaining cream and mix with the yogurt. Serve the muffins drizzled with the warm toffee sauce and a dollop of cream mixture.

MAKES 8 MEGA-MUFFINS / READY IN 40 MINUTES

Knob of butter, for greasing

250g | 9oz pitted dates, roughly chopped

5ml | 1 tsp bicarbonate of soda

50g | 2oz butter

225g | 8oz self-raising flour, sieved

10ml | 2 tsp baking powder

175g | 6oz light muscovado sugar

2 large eggs, lightly beaten

For the toffee sauce:

50g | 2oz butter

75g | 3oz light muscovado sugar

142ml carton double cream

6oml | 4 tbsp Greek yogurt

Vanilla bean muffins

Real vanilla pods are the fermented and dried seedpods of an orchid native to Mexico. They are expensive but the flavour is intense. When split in half, you can scrape out the hundreds of tiny vanilla seeds hidden within. However, look out for vanilla bean paste in the gourmet section of your supermarket – it's the perfect connoisseur's cheat. Alternatively, use real vanilla extract, but although it has a great authentic flavour, you'll have none of the characteristic seeds.

1 Heat the oven to 190°C/375°F/gas 5. Line 6 holes of a mega-muffin tin with paper muffin cases.
2 In a large bowl, combine the flour, sugar, baking powder and bicarbonate of soda.
3 In a jug, mix the egg, yogurt and vanilla together well.

4 Pour the wet ingredients over dry, add the melted butter and stir just to blend (just a few strokes, do not over mix).
5 Spoon the batter evenly into the prepared muffin cases. Sprinkle tops with vanilla or granulated sugar, if using, and bake for 25 minutes.

MAKES 6 MEGA-MUFFINS / READY IN 30 MINUTES

225g | 8oz plain flour

150g | 5oz golden caster sugar

15ml | 1 tbsp baking powder

1.25ml | ¼ tsp bicarbonate of soda

1 medium egg, beaten

250ml | 9 fl oz thick vanilla yogurt

22.5ml | 1½ tbsp vanilla extract or paste

100g | 3½oz butter, melted

30ml | 2 tbsp vanilla or granulated sugar

Dark chocolate truffle muffins

Every chocoholic's fantasy, these are wicked served with ice cream. Use a chocolate with 50 per cent cocoa solids (chocolate with 70 per cent cocoa solids would be too strong in this recipe).

MAKES 12 / READY IN 40 MINUTES

Knob of butter, for greasing

200g | 7oz dark chocolate, broken into squares

200g | 7oz unsalted butter, cubed

200g | 7oz self-raising flour

1.25ml | ¼ tsp baking powder

30ml | 2 tbsp cocoa powder

150g | 5oz golden caster sugar

150ml | 5fl oz milk

3 medium eggs

1 large chocolate caramel bar, cut into 12 pieces

For the truffle sauce:

100g | 3½oz each of dark and milk chocolate, broken into squares

15ml | 1 tbsp golden syrup

30ml | 2 tbsp milk or cream

1 Heat the oven to 180°C/350°F/gas 4. Grease a 12-hole muffin tin.
2 Put the chocolate and butter in a heatproof bowl. Microwave on medium (500w) for 2 minutes, stir and microwave for 2 more minutes until smooth.
3 In a large bowl, stir together the flour, baking powder, cocoa, and sugar.
4 In a jug, lightly mix together the milk and eggs with a fork, then stir into the dry ingredients, along with the melted chocolate. Mix to combine.
5 Put a spoonful of mixture into the base of each muffin hole and top with a slice of the chocolate caramel bar. Top with the remaining muffin mixture.
6 Bake for 18–20 minutes until risen.
7 For the truffle sauce, heat the chocolate with the golden syrup and milk or cream. Microwave on medium (500w) for 2 minutes, stir and cook for 1 more minute until the chocolate is melted and smooth.
8 Serve the muffins topped with caramel slices and drizzled with truffle sauce.

Tiramisu muffins

What a wonderful combination – chocolate, coffee and a boozy coffee mascarpone topping.

MAKES 12 / READY IN 40 MINUTES

375g | 12oz self-raising white flour

2.5ml | ½ tsp bicarbonate of soda

30ml | 2 tbsp cocoa powder

150g | 5oz light muscovado sugar

100g | 3½oz plain chocolate, coarsely grated

50g | 2oz white chocolate, coarsely grated

1 large egg

100 ml | 4fl oz sunflower oil

200ml | 7fl oz strong black coffee, cooled

200ml | 7fl oz skimmed milk

For the topping:

45ml | 3 tbsp coffee liqueur, optional

250g | 9oz mascarpone cheese

30ml | 2 tbsp milk

25g | 1oz unrefined golden icing sugar

15ml | 1 tbsp cocoa, sieved

1 Heat the oven to 200°C/400°F/gas 6. Line a 12-hole muffin tin with paper muffin cases.
2 Sift the flour, bicarbonate of soda and cocoa into a large bowl. Stir in the sugar and the plain and white chocolate.
3 In a large jug mix together the egg, sunflower oil, cooled black coffee and milk.
4 Pour the wet ingredients into the dry and stir together lightly until just combined. Do not over-mix.
5 Spoon the mixture into the paper cases and bake for 20 minutes until the muffins are well risen, firm yet springy and a cocktail stick inserted into the centre comes out clean.
6 Pierce several times with a cocktail stick and drizzle over the coffee liqueur, if using.
7 Mix together the mascarpone, milk and sieved icing sugar until smooth. Use a palette knife to spread over the cooled muffins. Dust with cocoa to finish.

Luxury lemon muffins

These lemon muffins taste fantastic straight from the oven. Make the limoncella syrup as an additional treat, but they taste really good without it too!

MAKES 8 MEGA-MUFFINS / READY IN 30 MINUTES

300g | 10oz self-raising flour

175g | 6oz golden caster sugar

150ml | 5fl oz natural yogurt

90ml | 6 tbsp skimmed milk

1 large egg

Finely grated zest and juice of 3 unwaxed lemons

100g | 3½oz unsalted butter

For the lemon syrup (optional):

Peeled and finely shredded zest and juice of 2 unwaxed lemons

125g | 4oz golden caster sugar

30ml | 2 tbsp limoncella (Italian lemon liqueur) (optional)

1 Heat the oven to 180°C/350°F/gas 4. Line 8 holes of a mega-muffin tin with paper muffin cases.
2 Sift the flour into a large bowl and add the sugar.
3 In a separate bowl, mix together the yogurt, milk, egg, grated lemon zest and juice.
4 Melt the butter in the microwave on high (850w) for 30 seconds, or melt in a pan. Add all the wet ingredients to the dry and gently stir.
5 Spoon the mixture into the prepared muffin tins. Bake for 20 minutes until the muffins are well risen, firm and a cocktail stick inserted into the centre comes out clean.
6 Meanwhile, make the lemon syrup, if you wish to. Put the shredded lemon zest and juice into a pan with the sugar. Heat gently, stir to dissolve the sugar, simmer for 5 minutes, then add the limoncella, if using.
7 Pour over a little warm syrup and zest while the muffins are warm.

Mini golden Victoria sandwiches

There's something good about an old-fashioned Victoria sandwich cake, perhaps because you get oodles of extra sweetness in the filling in what may otherwise be a plain cake. These modern mini sandwich cakes are packed with caramelly flavours, thanks to the variety of sugars this recipe uses.

MAKES 12 / READY IN 60 MINUTES

Knob of butter

225g | 8oz self-raising flour

5ml | 1 tsp baking powder

125g | 4oz light muscovado sugar

100g | 3½oz golden caster sugar

175g | 6oz butter, melted

10ml | 2 tsp vanilla extract

75 ml | 3fl oz skimmed milk

3 large eggs

For the filling:

200g | 7oz mascarpone cheese

150ml | 5fl oz Greek yogurt

30ml | 2 tbsp golden caster sugar

2.5ml | ½ tsp vanilla extract

60ml | 12 tsp strawberry jam

30ml | 2 tbsp unrefined golden icing sugar

1 Heat the oven to 190°C/375°F/gas 5. Grease a 12-hole muffin tin with butter.
2 Sieve the flour and baking powder into a bowl, then add both the sugars.
3 In a jug, mix together the melted butter, vanilla extract and milk, then add the eggs and mix with a fork to combine.
4 Pour the wet ingredients into the dry and stir together until thoroughly combined.
5 Spoon into the greased muffin tin and bake for 15 minutes until risen, firm yet springy and a cocktail stick inserted into the centre comes out clean.
6 Cool the muffins on a wire rack and cut each one in half horizontally.
7 Put the mascarpone cheese into a bowl with the Greek yogurt and stir until smooth. Stir in the sugar and vanilla extract. Sandwich the two muffin halves together with a dollop of jam and a smothering of the mascarpone cheese. Dust the tops with sieved icing sugar.

Fit for a Celebration

So many cakes are all about presentation and nothing about flavour. The worst offenders are shop-bought birthday cakes. Does anybody actually enjoy eating a slice? In my experience, children pick off the decorations and leave the rest. Big cakes can be daunting to make and sometimes the results are disappointing, so here I've used traditional cake recipes and adapted them to fit into muffin cases. They taste divine, look impressive and you can happily serve leftovers without them looking sad. Bake several batches and freeze ahead if you're catering for a crowd. Show them off in style by arranging them carefully on a series of thin cake boards in decreasing sizes, stacked up with cake pillars. Finish off with candles for a really memorable display!

Lavender and lemon birthday muffins

A hint of fresh lavender gives an old-fashioned, interesting fragrance to what would otherwise be a plain lemon muffin (though still good if lavender's not in season). It also makes a pretty decoration that's original yet hassle-free.

MAKES 6 MEGA-MUFFINS / READY IN 30 MINUTES

Knob of butter

5 heads of fresh lavender

150g | 5oz golden caster sugar

225g | 8oz self-raising flour

Finely grated zest and juice of 2 unwaxed lemons

2 medium eggs

150ml | 5fl oz sunflower oil

200ml | 7fl oz soured cream

For the icing:

75g | 3oz icing sugar

30-45ml | 2-3 tbsp lemon juice

3 heads of fresh lavender

1 Heat the oven to 190°C/375°F/gas 5. Butter 6 holes of a mega-muffin tin then line with paper muffin cases.
2 Strip the flowers from the lavender and put into a processor with the caster sugar. Blitz together.
3 Sift the flour into a large bowl.
4 In a jug, mix together the lemon zest and juice, eggs, sunflower oil, soured cream, and lavender sugar with a fork.
5 Pour the wet ingredients into the flour, add 100ml | 4fl oz water and stir together to combine.
6 Spoon into the paper muffin cases and bake for 20-25 minutes until well risen and firm.
7 Cool in the tin for 5 minutes, then loosen with a palette knife and cool on a wire rack.
8 Sieve the icing sugar into a bowl and stir in enough lemon juice to make a smooth pouring consistency. Spoon over the muffins.
9 Top with a piece of fresh lavender to serve. Finish with candles.

Squidgy chocolate Valentine's muffins

You can prepare these before you need them, then bake at the last minute to guarantee centres oozing with chocolate.

MAKES 12 / READY IN 40 MINUTES

175g | 6oz plain chocolate, broken into squares

175g | 6oz unsalted butter, cubed

4 medium eggs

4 egg yolks

75g | 3oz golden caster sugar

75g | 3oz plain flour, sieved

30ml | 2 tbsp icing sugar, sieved

1 Heat the oven to 190°C/375°F/gas 5. Line a 12-hole muffin tin with paper muffin cases.
2 Put the chocolate and butter in a heatproof bowl resting over a pan of simmering water and heat until melted. Stir once, then remove the bowl. Alternatively microwave on medium (500w) for 2 minutes, stir and cook for another 2 minutes.
3 Whisk the whole eggs, yolks and sugar with an electric mixer until very pale, foamy and doubled in volume. Pour in the melted chocolate mixture and gently fold in, followed by the flour. Pour into the paper cases.
4 Bake for 7 minutes until firm on the outside and squidgy in the centre.
5 To decorate, dust with icing sugar or cut out some small heart shapes from card. Lay these on top of the muffins, then sprinkle with sieved icing sugar. Carefully lift off the card hearts and serve.

Cook's tip: You can prepare these to the end of step 3, then chill in the fridge for up to 5 hours. Bake from chilled for 8 minutes to guarantee centres oozing with chocolate.

Simnel muffins with marzipan

Simnel cakes were traditionally made to test a girl's skills as a cook. Girls who worked in domestic service away from home were given the day off to bake on Mothering Sunday. Their gift was a home-made simnel cake – a spiced fruit cake with a surprise layer of marzipan. If the cake remained moist and tasty until Easter Sunday, she was regarded as a good cook.

MAKES 12 / READY IN 40 MINUTES

Knob of butter
225g | 8oz plain flour, sieved
10ml | 2 tsp baking powder
5ml | 1 tsp ground nutmeg
5ml | 1 tsp ground cinnamon
5ml | 1 tsp ground mixed spice
75g | 3oz golden caster sugar
75g | 3oz light muscovado sugar
250g | 9oz luxury mixed dried fruit
Finely grated zest and juice of 1 lemon
175g | 6oz butter, melted
3 medium eggs, lightly beaten
150ml | 5fl oz skimmed milk
350g | 12oz natural almond marzipan
90ml | 6 tbsp apricot glaze

1 Heat the oven to 180°C/350°F/gas 4. Butter a 12-hole large muffin tin.

2 Sift the flour, baking powder, nutmeg, cinnamon and mixed spice into a large bowl. Stir in the sugars and dried fruit.

3 Add the lemon zest and juice, melted butter, eggs and milk. Mix together until well combined.

4 Take half the marzipan and cut into 12 pieces. Roll each piece into a ball and flatten.

5 Put a generous spoonful of the simnel muffin mixture in each muffin hole. Top with a round of marzipan, then spoon on the rest of the muffin mixture.

6 Bake for 20 minutes until the cakes are risen, firm, pale golden and a cocktail stick inserted into the centre comes out clean.

7 Loosen the simnel muffins from the tin with a palette knife and cool on a wire rack.

8 Roll out the remaining marzipan and use a fluted 5cm | 2in cutter to cut out 12 flowers.

9 Brush the top of the muffins with apricot glaze and arrange the marzipan flowers on top. Flash under a hot grill to brown the marzipan or blitz with a hot gun (brazier) to caramelize it.

Halloween pumpkin toffee cakes

Just the job to serve up before or after Halloween – something tasty to make out of the scooped-out flesh from pumpkins. The recipe works equally well with hard squash like butternut if you want to make them throughout the year.

1 Pre-heat the oven to 180°C/350°F/gas 4. Line a 12-hole muffin tin with paper muffin cases.

2 Put the pumpkin flesh into a heatproof bowl with 15ml | 1 tbsp water. Microwave on high (850w) for 8 minutes. Or boil in a pan for 15 minutes, then drain.

3 Blend until smooth with a hand blender.

4 Put the oil, sugar and eggs in a large bowl and whisk together using a hand-held electric mixer until thick and pale.

5 Stir in the flour, bicarbonate of soda, ginger, cinnamon and mixed spice. Add the pumpkin purée.

6 Spoon the mixture into the paper cases and bake for 20 minutes.

7 Cool in the tin for 10 minutes, then transfer to a wire rack to cool.

8 Spread a spoonful of the Dulce de Leche over the top of each cooled cake and top with a dried apricot.

MAKES 12 / READY IN 50 MINUTES

500g | 1lb 2oz pumpkin flesh

250ml | 9 fl oz sunflower oil

300g | 11oz light muscovado sugar

3 large eggs

225g | 8oz self-raising flour

5ml | 1 tsp bicarbonate of soda

5ml | 1 tsp each ground ginger, cinnamon and mixed spice

345g jar Dulce de Leche (banoffee toffee)

12 ready-to-eat dried apricots

Cook's tip: Instead of fresh pumpkin, you could use a 450g can of cooked puréed pumpkin to save time.

Vanilla surprise christening cakes

These will be well received whether you're serving them up in the morning with coffee or in the afternoon for tea. The child-friendly flavours of vanilla with a surprise banana centre make an interesting alternative to a classic fruit cake. Banana chips are my chosen easiest decoration. However, if you're the creative type, you could pipe cute pastel-coloured icing decorations such as a bottle, silver spoon or the baby's initials.

1 Heat the oven to 180°C/350°F/gas 4. Line a 12-hole muffin tray with paper cases.

2 Sieve the flour, baking powder and bicarbonate of soda into a large bowl.

3 In a jug mix the buttermilk, vanilla extract, butter, sugar and eggs with a fork.

4 Pour the wet ingredients into the dry.

5 Half-fill the paper cases with muffin mixture and top with a spoonful of mashed banana. Top with the rest of the muffin

mixture and bake for 20 minutes until muffins are risen and firm and a cocktail stick inserted into the centre comes out clean.

6 For the frosting, beat together the cream cheese, butter and vanilla to combine. Sift in the icing sugar and mix together.

7 Spread the frosting onto the cooled muffins with a palette knife. Top each one with a banana chip or your chosen decoration.

MAKES 12 / READY IN 50 MINUTES

250g | 8oz plain flour

15ml | 1 tbsp baking powder

2.5ml | ½ tsp bicarbonate of soda

200ml | 7fl oz buttermilk

10ml | 2 tsp vanilla extract

125g | 4oz butter, melted

200g | 7oz golden caster sugar

3 large eggs

2 bananas, mashed with 5ml | 1 tsp lemon juice

For the frosting:

100g | 4oz low fat cream cheese

100g | 4oz butter, at room temperature

Drop of vanilla extract

125g | 4oz unrefined golden icing sugar

12 chewy banana chips

Christmas spice muffins with brandy butter frosting

I first made these one Christmas Eve. Friends were coming for tea and I realized at 3pm that I'd failed to make a traditional Christmas cake. The result: these mini cakes, lighter than the over-fruity, sometimes dry, seasonal cake. They're sure to become a new family tradition.

MAKES 15 / READY IN 1 HOUR

300g | 11oz mixed dried fruit

300ml | 10fl oz dark rum, sherry, brandy or Southern Comfort

250g | 9oz self-raising flour

2.5ml | ½ tsp baking powder

60ml | 4 tbsp ground mixed spice

5ml | 1 tsp ground ginger

225g | 8oz dark muscovado sugar

250g | 9oz butter, softened

4 medium eggs, lightly beaten

For the brandy butter frosting:

150g | 5oz unsalted butter, melted

150g | 5oz unrefined golden icing sugar

150g | 5oz cream cheese

15ml | 1 tbsp dark rum, sherry, brandy or Southern Comfort

About 45 edible silver balls

1 Put the dried fruit into a sealable container or large jar. Pour over the alcohol, reserving 15ml | 1 tbsp and heat in the microwave on high (850w) for 2 minutes to help plump up the fruit. Alternatively, put the fruit and alcohol into a pan and heat gently for 5 minutes.

2 Heat the oven to 170°C/325°F/gas 3. Line 15 holes in two muffin tins with paper muffin cases.

3 Pour half the mixture into a food processor and blend until smooth.

4 Put the flour, baking powder, mixed spice, ginger and sugar into a large bowl. Add the butter and eggs and stir together to combine.

5 Stir in the puréed fruit and the remaining soaked fruit and alcohol to combine evenly.

6 Spoon the mixture into the muffin cases and bake for 30 minutes until risen, firm and a cocktail stick inserted into the centre comes out clean.

7 Pierce the muffins in several places with a cocktail stick and drizzle over the remaining alcohol. Cool and store in an airtight container for up to one week.

8 To make the brandy butter frosting, put the butter and icing sugar into a food processor and blend until smooth. Add the cream cheese and alcohol and stir until combined. Chill until ready to serve the muffins.

9 Use a palette knife to spread the frosting over the muffins, then sprinkle each one with silver balls to decorate. Once topped, keep in the fridge for up to 1 week.

Cook's tip: The longer you leave the dried fruit and booze to soak, the more intense the flavour will be. Even an hour's soaking is a plus, but leaving it to macerate for up to a month makes the flavour really impressive!

White chocolate rose wedding muffins

There is no need to save these just for weddings. They taste great without the topping too.

1 Heat the oven to 200°C/400°F/gas 6. Line a 6-hole mega-muffin tin with paper muffin cases (or line a 12-hole regular muffin tin with paper muffin cases).
2 Sieve both flours, the baking powder and the bicarbonate of soda into a large bowl. Add the sugar, orange zest and juice, white chocolate and mix together.
3 In a large jug mix together the melted butter, eggs, milk and vanilla extract.
4 Pour the wet ingredients onto the dry ingredients and stir together to combine.
5 Spoon the mixture into the prepared tins and bake for 25 minutes. (Regular muffins should be baked for 15 minutes.)
6 Loosen muffins with a palette knife and cool on a wire rack. Pierce several times with a cocktail stick and pour over the sweet wine.
7 Put the chocolate and liquid glucose into a heatproof bowl, resting over a pan of simmering water. Heat for a few minutes until melted. Remove from the heat and sift in the icing sugar and stir together to form into a ball.
8 Cut the white chocolate icing into 6 pieces and mould each piece into a rose. Position on top of muffins to decorate.

MAKES 6 MEGA-MUFFINS, OR 12 REGULAR MUFFINS / READY IN 50 MINUTES

125g | 4oz plain flour
250g | 9oz self-raising flour
5ml | 1 tsp baking powder
2.5ml | ½ tsp bicarbonate of soda
200g | 7oz golden caster sugar
Grated zest and juice of 1 orange
100g | 3½oz white chocolate, chopped
200g | 7oz butter, melted
2 large eggs
200ml | 7fl oz skimmed milk
5ml | 1 tsp vanilla extract
150ml | 5fl oz sweet dessert wine

For the topping:
200g | 7oz white chocolate, chopped
142g tub liquid glucose
100g | 3½oz unrefined icing sugar

Amaretto and sugared almond muffins

Just want to say congratulations to celebrate a special occasion? These muffins fit the bill perfectly. Sugared almonds make a classy decoration and are available in a multitude of colours, from subtle pastels to glitzy metallics, so you're bound to find something to suit. These are also good for weddings.

1 Heat the oven to 190°C/375°F/gas 5. Butter a 6-hole mega-muffin tin and line with paper muffin cases.
2 Sieve the flour and bicarbonate of soda into a large bowl, then stir in the ground almonds, sugar, unbeaten egg whites, milk and softened butter. Stir to combine.
3 Spoon the mixture into the paper muffin cases and bake for 20 minutes until well risen and firm.
4 Drizzle each muffin with the amaretto liqueur.
5 Sieve the icing sugar into a bowl and stir in the water and almond extract to make a smooth icing. Spoon the icing over each muffin. Top with a sugared almond to decorate.

MAKES 6 MEGA-MUFFINS / READY IN 40 MINUTES

Knob of butter
125g | 4oz self-raising flour
2.5ml | ½ tsp bicarbonate of soda
125g | 4oz ground almonds
125g | 4oz golden caster sugar
3 egg whites
150ml | 5fl oz skimmed milk
125g | 4oz butter, softened
45ml | 3 tbsp Amaretto liqueur

For the topping:
175g | 6oz white icing sugar
30ml | 2 tbsp water
2.5ml | ½ tsp almond extract
6 sugared almonds

Devil's food birthday muffins

Little chocolate cakes that are light enough to enjoy as a birthday treat and gooey enough to feel indulgent.

1 Pour the milk into a jug and squeeze in the lemon juice. Stir and leave for a few minutes to sour. Heat the oven to 190°C/375°F/gas 5.

2 Put the butter and half the sugar into a large bowl and use an electric mixer to cream together until pale, light and fluffy.

3 Add the rest of the sugar, then gradually whisk in the eggs.

4 Sieve half of the flour, bicarbonate of soda, baking powder and cocoa onto the mixture and pour over half the soured milk. Whisk together, then whisk in the rest of the flour and milk.

5 Spoon the mixture into the prepared muffin tins and bake for 20 minutes until they are well risen, firm yet springy and a cocktail stick inserted into the centre comes out clean.

6 Pierce the muffins several times with a cocktail stick and drizzle a little Southern Comfort onto each one, if using.

7 For the topping, put the sugar, cream of tartar and egg whites into a large heatproof bowl over a pan of simmering water. Use a hand-held electric whisk to whisk continuously until the mixture is glossy, holds its shape and looks like meringue. This will take 3–4 minutes.

8 Spread the frosting over the top of the cakes with a palette knife. Drag a vegetable peeler over the chocolate to make curls and sprinkle over the top of the cakes.

Cook's tip: To make a personalized chocolate decoration, break up the chocolate and microwave in a bowl on medium (500w) for 2 minutes until just softened. Spoon the melted chocolate into a paper piping bag. Line a tray with baking parchment. Snip off the end of the piping bag and gently squeeze the chocolate onto the parchment-lined tray into your chosen shape. Chill for at least 1 hour. Carefully ease a palette knife between the chocolate and the paper to release and position on top of each cake.

MAKES 20 REGULAR MUFFINS / READY IN 1 HOUR

375 ml | 12fl oz skimmed milk
Juice of ½ a lemon
175g | 6oz unsalted butter, at room temperature
375g | 13oz caster sugar
3 medium eggs
350g | 12oz plain flour
5ml | 1 tsp bicarbonate of soda
10ml | 2 tsp baking powder
25g | 1oz cocoa powder
45ml | 3 tbsp Southern Comfort, optional

For the frosting:
350g | 12oz caster sugar
2.5ml | ½ tsp cream of tartar
2 medium egg whites
100g | 3½oz plain chocolate, to decorate

Anniversary pistachio and rose water muffins

An intriguing recipe with a delicate flavour. Why not serve these on a large plate or tray made from the material traditionally associated with each year's celebration.

MAKES 12 REGULAR MUFFINS / READY IN 35 MINUTES

225g | 8oz plain flour
15ml | 1 tbsp baking powder
125g | 4oz golden caster sugar
100g | 3½oz pistachios, roughly chopped in a food processor
100g | 3½oz butter, melted
150ml | 5fl oz soured cream
125g | 4oz runny honey
2 medium eggs

For the rose water icing:
200g | 7oz white icing sugar
5ml | 1 tsp culinary rose water
45ml | 3 tbsp boiling water
Crystallised rose petals, to decorate

1 Heat the oven to 190°C/375°F/gas 5. Line a 12-hole muffin tin with paper muffin cases.
2 Sift the flour and baking powder into a bowl and stir in the sugar and pistachios.
3 In a jug mix the melted butter, soured cream, runny honey and eggs with a fork.
4 Pour the wet ingredients onto the dry and stir together until just smooth.
5 Pour the mixture equally into the muffin cases and bake for 20 minutes until risen, firm and springy and a cocktail stick inserted into the centre comes out clean.
6 Sieve the icing sugar into a bowl, add the rose water and 30ml | 2 tbsp of boiling water. Mix together until it is the consistency of single cream. Add a little more water if needed.
7 Spoon the rose water icing on top of the muffins. Leave to set, then sprinkle over a few rose petals to serve.

Internationally Inspired

The interesting thing about baking is that although everyone loves tucking into warm, home-made goodies worldwide, cooks' methods vary greatly. My starting point for any recipe tends to be what's quickest and easiest, which is why I love traditional American muffins. However, sometimes for an authentic continental flavour a little extra effort is required. This chapter features ten of my favourite recipes from all corners of the globe, several of them including classic techniques that many purists could dispute make them worthy of being called a muffin. But I reckon if they're cooked in a muffin tin they have every right to be included.

American cranberry and orange muffins

The tanginess of cranberries gives a refreshing taste to these muffins, and is complemented by the orange zest.

MAKES 6 MEGA MUFFINS / READY IN 30 MINUTES

125g | 5oz fresh or frozen cranberries
25g | 1oz icing sugar
250g | 9oz plain flour
10ml | 2 tsp baking powder
150g | 5oz golden caster sugar
Finely grated zest of 1 large orange
1 large egg
250ml | 8fl oz milk
50g | 2oz unsalted butter, melted
Icing sugar, sieved for dusting

1 Heat the oven to 200°C/400°F/gas 6. Line a 6-hole mega-muffin tin with paper muffin cases.
2 Toss the cranberries in the icing sugar to coat.
3 Sift the flour and baking powder into a large bowl. Stir in the sugar, orange zest and cranberries.
4 In a large jug mix together the egg, milk and butter. Add the wet ingredients to the dry ingredients and gently stir everything together until just combined.
5 Spoon into the muffin cases and bake for 15-20 minutes until well risen and firm.
6 Cool on a wire rack and dust with icing sugar to serve.

Cook's tip: Cranberries are only available for a short season, so stock up whilst they're in the shops and freeze for up to 6 months. Alternatively, use 100g | 3½oz of dried cranberries which are available all year. Omit the icing sugar.

American blueberry and soured cream muffins

Blueberries may sometimes be pricey but they're worth it. They're considered a superfood as they're so high in vitamin C. But don't give yourself a false sense of security – it's no excuse for gorging on these delicious muffins as they do also contain butter and sugar; a sprinkling of fresh blueberries over natural yogurt with a handful of oats would be healthier!

MAKES 6 MEGA-MUFFINS / READY IN 30 MINUTES

200g | 7oz plain flour
2.5ml | ¼ tsp bicarbonate of soda
10ml | 2 tsp baking powder
100g | 3½oz golden caster sugar
Pinch of salt
75g | 3oz butter, melted
200ml | 7fl oz soured cream
1 large egg
200g | 7oz blueberries

1 Heat the oven to 200°C/400°F/gas 6. Line a 6-hole mega-muffin tin with paper cases.
2 Sieve the flour, bicarbonate of soda and baking powder into a bowl. Add the sugar and salt.
3 Pour the butter, soured cream and egg into a jug and mix together with a fork.
4 Pour the wet ingredients into the dry ingredients and add the blueberries. Gently stir everything together until just mixed.
5 Spoon the mixture into the muffin cases and bake for 15-20 minutes until they are well risen and firm.

French madeleines

These are dinky little buns that keep really well. The mix here actually improves if it's made ahead of time and chilled before baking.

MAKES 18 PATTY TIN SIZED MUFFINS / READY IN 1 HOUR

150g | 5oz unsalted butter, melted

Plain flour, for dusting

4 medium eggs

125g | 4oz caster sugar

Finely grated zest of 1 lemon

125g | 4oz plain white flour

5ml | 1 tsp baking powder

Pinch of salt

30ml | 2 tbsp icing sugar, for dusting

1 Brush 18 holes in patty tins with 25g | 1oz of the melted butter and leave for a few minutes, then dust with flour.
2 Whisk the eggs, sugar and lemon zest in a bowl with an electric whisk until they are pale, creamy and thick enough to leave a trail when the beaters are lifted.
3 Sift in half the flour with the baking powder and salt. Carefully pour half the melted butter around the sides of the bowl and gently fold in. Repeat with remaining butter and flour and gently fold in. Cover and chill for 45 minutes. (This gives madeleines their characteristic dense texture.)
4 Heat the oven to 220°C/425°F/gas 7. Pour the mixture into the prepared tins.
5 Bake the madeleines for 10 minutes or until well risen and golden. Ease out of the tins with a palette knife and cool on a wire rack. Dust with icing sugar.

Greek lemon syrup cakes

Here's semolina in a whole new guise – added to flour with almonds to add a scrumptious mealy texture to a dessert muffin. Drenched in fragrant cardamom and orange flower syrup, these are really special.

MAKES 8 MEGA-MUFFINS / READY IN 35 MINUTES

125g | 4oz unsalted butter, softened, plus extra for greasing

100g | 3½oz golden caster sugar

Finely grated zest and juice of 2 lemons

2 medium eggs

125g | 4oz semolina

10ml | 2 tsp baking powder

100g | 3½oz ground almonds

For the syrup:

Juice and peel of 1 orange, removed with a vegetable peeler and cut into needle shreds

8 cardamom pods, crushed

1 cinnamon stick, broken into pieces

300g | 10oz golden caster sugar

200ml | 7fl oz water

Juice of ½ lemon

30ml | 2 tbsp orange flower water

1 Heat the oven to 200°C/400°F/gas 6. Grease 8 mega-muffin tins with butter.
2 Put the butter and sugar into the bowl of a food processor and whiz together until pale, light and fluffy.
3 Add the lemon zest and juice, eggs, semolina, baking powder and ground almonds and whiz until smooth.
4 Spoon the mixture into the prepared tins and bake for 15 minutes until just firm. Leave in the tins for 5 minutes, then loosen with a palette knife and put the cakes onto a shallow tray to cool.
5 To make the syrup, put the orange shreds into a pan and add the orange juice. Add the cardamom pods, cinnamon stick, sugar, water and lemon juice.
6 Heat gently to dissolve the sugar, then boil rapidly for 3–5 minutes until syrupy. Remove from the heat and add the orange flower water.
7 Pour the syrup over the cakes to drench them, leaving excess in the tray. Cool, cover and chill. Serve drizzled with extra syrup and a dollop of Greek yogurt.

Turkish coffee and nut muffins

Really strong, freshly made espresso coffee gives these muffins an authentic flavour, although you could use 30ml/2 tbsp of instant espresso granules if you're not a fresh coffee fiend.

MAKES 8 REGULAR MUFFINS / READY IN 30 MINUTES

175g | 6oz plain flour

10ml | 2 tsp baking powder

25g | 1oz toasted hazelnuts, blended until ground

175g | 6oz light muscovado sugar

100g | 3½oz butter, melted

90ml | 6 tbsp very strong espresso coffee

3 medium eggs

25g | 1oz toasted hazelnuts, chopped

1 Heat the oven to 180°C/350°F/gas 4. Line a 12-hole muffin tin with 8 paper muffin cases.
2 Sift the flour into a bowl with the baking powder. Add the toasted ground hazelnuts and sugar.
3 In a large jug mix together the melted butter, coffee liquid and eggs with a fork.
4 Pour the wet ingredients into the dry and stir together until well combined.
5 Spoon into the paper muffin cases and sprinkle over the chopped hazelnuts.
6 Bake for 20 minutes or until well risen and firm.

Italian pine nut and almond muffins

You may already use pine nuts to make pesto or in salads, but they're also gorgeous in sweet dishes. The light olive oil works really well in this, too.

MAKES 12 REGULAR MUFFINS / READY IN 30 MINUTES

Knob of butter, to grease

175g | 6oz plain flour

10ml | 2 tsp baking powder

50g | 2oz pine nuts, blended in a processor until ground

50g | 2oz ground almonds

125g | 4oz golden caster sugar

Finely grated zest of 1 small lemon

250ml | 9fl oz soured cream

2 medium eggs

75 ml | 3fl oz light olive oil

25g | 1oz pine nuts

25g | 1oz whole almonds, chopped

30ml | 2 tbsp icing sugar, to dust

1 Heat the oven to 180°C/350°F/gas 4. Grease a 12-hole muffin tin.
2 Sieve the flour and baking powder into a large bowl. Stir in the ground pine nuts, ground almonds, caster sugar and lemon zest.
3 Pour the soured cream into a jug and add the eggs and olive oil. Mix together with a fork.
4 Gently stir the wet ingredients to the dry to combine.
5 Spoon the muffin mixture into the greased muffin cases. Sprinkle over the pine nuts and chopped almonds.
6 Bake for 12 minutes or until a cocktail stick inserted into the centre comes out clean.
7 Cool on a wire rack and dust with sieved icing sugar to finish.

French tarte tatin

Enjoy this warm as a perfect dessert or treat with a coffee.

MAKES 6 REGULAR MUFFINS / READY IN 1 HOUR

1 For the topping, melt the butter over a low heat in a frying pan, add the 100g/3½oz sugar and heat until melted.
2 Add the apples, cover and leave for 5 minutes without turning, then gently stir and cook for a further 5 minutes until the sugar has caramelized to a rich golden brown.
3 Heat the oven to 180°C/350°F/gas 4. Line a 6-hole muffin tin with paper muffin cases.
4 For the base, sift the flour and baking powder into a bowl. Add the sugar and stir to combine.

5 Put the crème fraîche, eggs, butter, water and vanilla extract into a jug and stir together using a fork.
6 Pour the wet ingredients onto the dry and stir gently to combine.
7 Arrange the caramelized apple slices in the base of each muffin case. Spoon over the muffin mixture and bake for 20 minutes until the muffins are well risen and springy.
8 Upturn muffins onto serving plate and peel away the paper muffin cases.

For the topping:

50g | 2oz butter

100g | 3½oz golden caster sugar

750g | 1lb 11oz eating apples, peeled, quartered, cored and sliced, and tossed in 30ml | 2 tbsp lemon juice

For the base:

225g | 8oz plain flour

10ml | 2 tsp baking powder

175g | 6oz golden caster sugar

250g | 9oz crème fraîche

2 medium eggs

75g | 3oz butter, melted

100ml | 4fl oz water

5ml | 1 tsp vanilla extract

Jamaican Bun

My family adores this. We first discovered it sold as large sweet bread loaves in West Indian bakeries. A kind midwife revealed the recipe for a home-made version whilst I was in labour with my third child! In the mêlée I lost that original recipe but have since devised this one myself. Traditionally served at Easter time, but great anytime served with slices of Cheddar cheese.

MAKES 12 REGULAR MUFFINS / READY IN 1 HOUR

1 Heat the oven to 190°C/375°F/gas 5. Grease a 12-hole muffin tin with butter
2 Sift the flour, bicarbonate of soda, mixed spice and nutmeg into a large bowl. Add the sugar and sultanas.
3 Pour in the butter, eggs, stout, milk and lemon juice and stir well together to make a soft dropping consistency.

4 Spoon the mixture into the buttered muffin tin and bake for 40 minutes or until a cocktail stick inserted into the centre comes out clean.

Knob of butter, to grease

250g | 9oz self-raising flour

2.5ml | ½ tsp bicarbonate of soda

5ml | 1 tsp ground mixed spice

2.5ml | ½ tsp ground nutmeg

200g | 7oz light muscovado sugar

150g | 5oz sultanas

125g | 4oz butter, melted

2 medium eggs, lightly beaten

100ml | 4fl oz stout

100ml | 4fl oz milk

15ml | 1 tbsp lemon juice

Spanish orange and almond muffins

You may take one look at this and flinch at the thought of boiling and blending an orange at the beginning of this recipe. I urge you to give it a try and I think you'll agree that the extra effort is rewarded by the moist texture of the finished muffin and improved even more when they're drenched in orange syrup.

MAKES 12 REGULAR MUFFINS / READY IN 1 HOUR

2 unwaxed oranges, washed
125g | 4oz ground almonds
175g | 6oz golden caster sugar
10ml | 2 tsp baking powder
75g | 3oz butter, melted, plus extra for greasing
4 medium eggs

For the orange syrup:
225g | 8oz golden caster sugar
150ml | 5fl oz orange juice
100ml | 4fl oz water

1 Pierce the oranges several times with a sharp knife and put into a heatproof bowl. Cover with boiling water. Microwave on high (850w) for 20 minutes until the orange is really tender. Alternatively, put the oranges into a pan, cover with boiling water and simmer for 1 hour until tender.

2 Put the whole drained oranges into a food processor and blend together until they turn into a smooth purée.

3 Heat the oven to 170°C/325°F/gas 3. Grease a 12-hole muffin tin.

4 Put the almonds, sugar and baking powder into a bowl. Pour in the melted butter, puréed oranges and eggs and mix together thoroughly.

5 Spoon into the prepared tins and bake for 40 minutes or until a cocktail stick inserted into the centre comes out clean.

6 For the syrup, put the sugar, orange juice and water into a pan. Boil for 15 minutes until the liquid turns syrupy.

7 Loosen the warm cakes with a palette knife and put onto serving plates. Pour over the syrup to serve. Lovely served with a generous dollop of crème fraîche.

Canadian maple syrup and pecan

I was once was lucky enough to see sap-collecting from a maple tree in snowy North America. This liquid is boiled so that the water evaporates but the sugar stays, leaving a divinely unctuous sticky syrup. This is a wonderful natural sweet product that deserves respect.

MAKES 12 REGULAR MUFFINS / READY IN 35 MINUTES

225g | 8oz plain flour
10ml | 2 tsp baking powder
100g | 3½oz light muscovado sugar
125g | 5oz pecans, roughly chopped
100g | 3½oz butter, melted
200g | 7oz maple syrup
2 medium eggs
60ml | 4 tbsp maple syrup, to glaze

1 Heat the oven to 190°C/375°F/gas 5. Line a 12-hole muffin tin with paper muffin cases.

2 Sift the flour and baking powder into a bowl and stir in the sugar and pecans.

3 Mix the melted butter, maple syrup and eggs in a jug with a fork.

4 Pour the wet ingredients onto the dry and stir together until just smooth.

5 Pour the mixture into the muffin cases and bake for 20 minutes until risen, firm and springy and a cocktail stick inserted into the centre comes out clean.

6 Brush the warm muffins with maple syrup.

Nutritional Values (per serving)

KEY

All values are per muffin

Figures in ( ) indicate the number of muffins each recipe makes

Tr indicates that a small trace of the nutrient is present

Recipe	Energy (kcal)	Fat (g)	SFA (g)	Carbs (g)	Fibre (g)	Vegetarain (●)
Brilliant for Breakfast						
Granary honey muffins (9)	182	9	1	22	2	●
Five-seed muffins (12)	188	9	1	29	6	●
Apricot and oat muffins (12)	250	9	1	39	3	●
Wholemeal apple (12)	200	8	1	29	2	●
English muffins (8)	250	6	3	45	2	●
English muffins (10)	200	5	3	36	1	●
Bacon, cheese and maple syrup (8)	164	7	3	20	1	
Muesli muffins (9)	240	12	2	32	2	●
Smoked salmon and soured cream (9)	190	10	2	20	1	
Smoked salmon and soured cream (24)	176	8	2	20	1	
Marmalade orange muffins (12)	200	8	1	31	2	●
Muscovado, bran and banana (12)	170	7	1	25	3	●
Children's Choice						
Chocolate chip muffins (12)	160	9	3	19	Tr	●
Crunchy peanut butter muffins (24)	94	6	1	10	1	●
Banana and honey muffins (24)	60	3	Tr	8	Tr	●
Chocolate muffins (17)	180	8	4	25	Tr	●
Coconut muffins (24)	90	4	2	12	1	●
Lemon curd muffins (12)	190	7	1	33	1	●
Pink fairy muffins (12)	160	5	1	29	Tr	●
Marbled soccer muffins (12)	190	9	3	24	Tr	●
Jam surprise muffins (12)	147	6	1	24	1	●
Squashed fly muffins (12)	140	5	1	21	Tr	●
Classic Combinations						
Lemon and poppy seed muffins (12)	240	12	2	30	1	●
Sticky ginger and golden syrup muffins (12)	200	9	1	29	1	●

Recipe	Energy (kcal)	Fat (g)	SFA (g)	Carbs (g)	Fibre (g)	Vegetarain (●)
Buttery vanilla muffins (12)	270	11	7	41	1	●
Apple and cinnamon crumble muffins (12)	170	6	1	28	1	●
Mincemeat and rum muffins (12)	250	6	3	46	1	●
Cheese and chutney muffins (12)	200	9	6	23	1	●
Cappuccino and chocolate chip (12)	280	13	8	40	1	●
Banana and toffee muffins (12)	220	7	4	39	1	●
Carrot and cream cheese muffins (8)	536	32	13	59	1	●
Chocolate brownie muffins (12)	390	22	13	45	Tr	●
Something Savoury						
Spicy tex-mex muffins (12)	240	22	6	6	Tr	●
Walnut, leek and bacon muffins (12)	220	20	9	6	1	
Mushroom and sunblush tomato muffins (12)	170	8	2	20	1	●
Roast pepper and mozzarella cheese muffins (9)	230	10	3	29	2	●
Italian pizza muffins (12)	200	11	4	18	1	
Polenta and cheese muffins (9)	170	4	2	27	1	●
Feta and olive muffins (12)	220	13	4	20	1	●
Pesto muffins (9)	280	18	4	20	1	●
Prawn and peppadew muffins (12)	200	13	5	17	1	
Cheese, sage and onion muffins (12)	170	10	3	16	1	●
Slimline Selection						
Blueberry and oat muffins (8)	260	7	1	45	3	●
Low-fat berry and apple muffins (12)	112	1	Tr	24	6	●
Low-fat yoghurt and sour cherry (12)	130	Tr	Tr	30	1	●
Ricotta and spinach (12)	160	14	7	2	Tr	●
Cinnamon English muffins (10)	200	5	3	37	1	●
Wholemeal yoghurt and malted raisin (12)	130	Tr	Tr	30	1	●

Recipe	Energy (kcal)	Fat (g)	SFA (g)	Carbs (g)	Fibre (g)	Vegetarian (•)
Butter-free chocolate and prune (11)	213	6	1	49	2	•
Tangy cranberry (12)	180	5	3	34	1	•
Egg and bacon treats (9)	210	17	9	1	0	
Low-fat sultana bran and English muffins (10)	200	3	2	38	5	•

Special Diets

Recipe	Energy (kcal)	Fat (g)	SFA (g)	Carbs (g)	Fibre (g)	Vegetarian (•)
Cornmeal scones (9)	190	6	3	29	1	•
Carrot and pineapple muffins (12)	270	13	2	38	1	•
Buckwheat and apple muffins (12)	240	6	1	44	2	•
Gooseberry and almond muffins (12)	300	17	2	33	3	•
Sweet potato muffins (9)	280	2	2	41	1	•
Bran, date and prune muffins (12)	210	8	1	30	3	•
Oatmeal and raspberry muffins (12)	200	5	1	37	1	•
Lactose-free courgette muffins (12)	310	15	2	44	1	•
Herb popovers (6)	150	4	1	21	1	•
Sugar-free double-corn muffins (9)	200	9	1	25	1	•

Scones

Recipe	Energy (kcal)	Fat (g)	SFA (g)	Carbs (g)	Fibre (g)	Vegetarian (•)
English afternoon tea scones (8)	280	13	8	40	1	•
Malted grain scones (8)	150	6	3	23	2	•
Sunflower seed and honey scones (8)	230	12	6	27	2	•
Cheddar and thyme scones (8)	170	8	5	22	1	•
Carrot and raisin scones (8)	210	6	4	37	1	•
Wholemeal scone round (6)	220	8	5	35	3	•
Vanilla and buttermilk scones (8)	200	6	4	32	1	•
Buttermilk drop scones (6)	220	8	3	32	1	•
Blueberry cinnamon scones (8)	220	6	4	37	1	•
Cranberry and walnut scones (8)	250	10	4	37	2	•

Time to Indulge

Recipe	Energy (kcal)	Fat (g)	SFA (g)	Carbs (g)	Fibre (g)	Vegetarian (•)
Stem ginger muffins (6)	353	15	9	50	7	•
Strawberries and cream (6)	562	27	11	76	2	•
Mixed nut and muscovado muffins (4)	677	37	3	81	5	•
Coconut, carrot, pecan and pineapple muffins (6)	734	40	11	90	5	•
Sticky toffee and date muffins (8)	503	23	14	75	2	•
Vanilla bean muffins (6)	400	17	10	59	1	•

Recipe	Energy (kcal)	Fat (g)	SFA (g)	Carbs (g)	Fibre (g)	Vegetarian (•)
Dark chocolate truffle muffins (12)	520	30	18	56	1	•
Tiramisu muffins (12)	420	23	10	50	1	•
Luxury lemon muffins (8)	405	12	7	71	1	•
Mini golden Victoria sandwiches (12)	373	21	13	43	1	•

Fit for a Celebration

Recipe	Energy (kcal)	Fat (g)	SFA (g)	Carbs (g)	Fibre (g)	Vegetarian (•)
Lavender and lemon birthday muffins (6)	534	28	7	69	1	•
Squidgy chocolate Valentine's muffins (12)	280	20	12	20	Tr	•
Simnel muffins with marzipan (12)	436	18	8	67	2	•
Halloween Pumpkin toffee cakes (12)	450	22	3	60	1	•
Vanilla surprise christening cakes (12)	410	21	13	53	1	•
Christmas spice muffins with brandy butter frosting (15)	530	29	18	55	1	•
White chocolate rose wedding muffins (6)	1065	46	27	153	2	•
White chocolate rose wedding muffins (12)	533	23	14	77	1	•
Amaretto and sugared almond muffins (6)	585	29	12	73	2	•
Devil's food birthday muffins (20)	320	10	6	56	1	•
Anniversary pistachio and rose water muffins (12)	350	13	5	57	1	•

Internationally Inspired

Recipe	Energy (kcal)	Fat (g)	SFA (g)	Carbs (g)	Fibre (g)	Vegetarian (•)
American cranberry and orange muffins (6)	352	9	5	66	2	•
American blueberry and soured cream muffins (6)	376	19	11	45	2	•
French madeleines (18)	120	8	5	8	Tr	•
Greek lemon syrup cakes (8)	470	22	10	65	1	•
Turkish coffee and nut muffins (8)	310	15	8	40	1	•
Italian pine nut and almond muffins (12)	290	19	5	26	1	•
French tarte tatin (6)	690	36	23	90	1	•
Jamaican bun (12)	240	10	6	34	1	•
Spanish orange and almond muffins (12)	280	13	4	38	2	•
Canadian maple syrup and pecan (12)	300	15	5	38	1	•

Index

Recipes are for American muffins unless otherwise indicated. Page numbers in **bold** denote illustrations.